Vera Brittain
and the
First World War

Vera Brittain and the First World War

The Story of *Testament of Youth*

Mark Bostridge

BLOOMSBURY

LONDON • NEW DELHI • NEW YORK • SYDNEY

First published in Great Britain 2014

Copyright © Mark Bostridge, 2014

The moral right of the author has been asserted
Quotations from Vera Brittain copyright Mark Bostridge and Timothy
Brittain-Catlin, Literary Executors for the Estate of Vera Brittain 1970

Bloomsbury Publishing Plc
50 Bedford Square
London WC1B 3DP

www.bloomsbury.com

Bloomsbury is a trademark of Bloomsbury Publishing Plc

Bloomsbury Publishing, London, New Delhi, New York and Sydney

A CIP record for this book is available from the British Library.

ISBN: 978-1-4081-8844-6
Export Trade Paperback ISBN: 978-1-4729-1857-4
ePub ISBN: 978-1-4081-8845-3
ePdf ISBN: 978-1-4081-8846-0
10 9 8 7 6 5 4 3 2

Typeset by Fakenham Prepress Solutions, Fakenham, Norfolk NR21 8NN

Printed and bound in Great Britain by CPI Group (UK) Ltd, Croydon
CR0 4YY

For Shirley Williams
and for
Sam and Nat Honey
— the next generation

Vera Brittain in 1917

All sorrows can be borne if you put them into a story or tell a story about them.
Karen Blixen (Isak Dinesen)

Contents

List of Illustrations

Text

Plates

Foreword

In the deepening gloom of an autumn evening, with only the newly lit street lamps puncturing the encroaching darkness, a young woman called Vera Brittain walks up Whitehall in central London. She makes her way through the jubilant mass of celebrating crowds, past the spot where Edwin Lutyens's Cenotaph will be unveiled exactly two years later. It is 11 November 1918. The guns had fallen silent at 11 o'clock that morning, marking the end of a World War that had lasted for more than four years, at a cost in lives, to the British Empire alone, of nearly a million men.

Vera Brittain could not share in those feelings of celebration. The end of the war had come too late for her and for her male contemporaries. Instead, the dominant emotions she felt that day were ones of isolation and loneliness, born of the sudden full realisation that everything that had hitherto made up her life had vanished with the loss of four young men killed in the war: her fiancé, Roland Leighton, two close friends, Victor Richardson and Geoffrey Thurlow, and, finally, her beloved only brother Edward. Years later, in a letter to a friend, Brittain relived the sensations of that day. She related them to her recurrent fear 'of being left alone again in a world where no one cares *with* me for the things I care for, or understands why I should care for them – a blind, empty, soundless world like the world for me on the first Armistice Day'.

Vera Brittain's sense of alienation on that November evening in 1918 is portrayed with heartrending anguish in her most famous book, *Testament of Youth*, her classic memoir of the war years, during which she postponed her university education at Oxford and served as a Voluntary Aid Detachment nurse in hospitals in London, Malta and France. First published in Britain and the United States in 1933, the book instantly became a bestseller on both sides of the Atlantic. At the end of the 1970s it became a bestseller again when it was republished in a new paperback edition by Virago Press, and triumphantly adapted for an award-winning BBC Television series. To Shirley Williams, Vera Brittain's daughter, the republication of the book allowed a new generation more distant from the First World War 'to discover the anguish and pain' of young people like her mother and her male contemporaries, and, in discovering, to understand.

More than three decades on from its reappearance, as we commemorate the centenary of the First World War, deprived of the living witness of the men and women who struggled through those four years of conflict, *Testament of Youth* is still helping us to understand. It tells the reader in highly personal terms about the lasting impact of war on ordinary people's lives, and issues a warning to succeeding generations about the dangers of succumbing out of naive idealism to the false glamour of war. Vera Brittain called *Testament of Youth* a 'passionate plea for peace', which attempts to show 'without any polite disguise, the agony of war …

and its destructiveness to the human race'. The book is arguably the greatest work of love, loss and remembrance to emerge from the First World War. To my mind there is nothing else in the prose literature of the war that so eloquently and movingly conveys the suffering and bereavement inflicted on the generation of 1914.

And while it is regrettable that other fine books by women about the war are not better known, *Testament of Youth* is the only book by a woman to find a place in the British canon of Great War literature, alongside works by such male writers as Edmund Blunden, Robert Graves and Siegfried Sassoon. Brittain was intent on offering her book as a corrective to masculine accounts, which emphasised women's passive suffering during the war instead of their active service. To Brittain, the women of the war generation had helped to bridge the gulf between their Victorian forbears, 'who merely endured', and 'the 20th century women, who pull down and change things, adventure and construct'.

Paradoxically, the war that devastated Brittain's youth also helped to create her as a writer. Vera Brittain spent much of her writing life describing the war and its impact, in a wide variety of literary genres: diaries, letters, poetry, fiction, memoir, journalism, polemic (the only comparable male writer of the war in this respect, constantly rewriting his experiences, is Sassoon). But it is *Testament of Youth* that stands alone as her lasting contribution to history and to literature.

In this short book I have tried to present in concise form the outline of Vera Brittain's First World War experiences, alongside chapters about the writing of

Testament of Youth, and its eventual translation to television; to the world of dance (as the inspiration for Kenneth MacMillan's ballet *Gloria*); and, in 2015, to the big screen, in the feature film adaptation of the book, starring Alicia Vikander and Kit Harington.

The standard full-length biography remains *Vera Brittain: A Life* by Paul Berry and myself, first published 20 years ago (I provide some details of our unlikely, though ultimately successful, collaboration in a closing piece about the biographical mystery surrounding Edward Brittain's last days, prior to his death in action in northern Italy, in June 1918). But this new book draws on material about the complex evolution of *Testament of Youth* that was not available at the time of the researching and writing of the biography. I hope it will serve as an initial port of call for those coming to Vera Brittain for the first time, perhaps as a result of seeing the film, or of studying *Testament of Youth* at school or university. I hope also that it may stimulate further critical work about the place of *Testament of Youth* in First World War literature.

I am deeply indebted to two people without whose friendship I would never have studied Vera Brittain's life and work: Rebecca Williams and Timothy Brittain-Catlin. I appreciate the fact that they have never so much as broached the subject of whether I am ever going to stop writing about their grandmother. I am immensely grateful to Shirley Williams, David Leighton (Roland Leighton's nephew) and Shiona Robotham (Victor Richardson's niece), who have been generous and supportive over many years. I would like to pay tribute to the memory of Paul Berry, a close friend of Vera

Brittain's for 28 years, and her one-time literary executor, who worked tirelessly for Vera Brittain's reputation in the 30 years after her death.

I'd also like to take this opportunity to salute the actresses who have portrayed Vera Brittain in various productions since 1979: Cheryl Campbell, Rohan McCullough (whose one-woman show toured Britain for over a quarter of a century), Amanda Root, Katherine Manners and Alicia Vikander.

The late Elaine Morgan, who died in 2013, was enormously helpful in providing me with her recollections of the 1979 television adaptation of *Testament of Youth*.

Rosie Alison, producer with David Heyman of the film of *Testament of Youth*, kindly allowed me to visit filming on many occasions over the seven-week shoot. Vera Brittain's family and her Estate owe her a great deal, for without her passionate commitment the film would never have gone before the cameras. I personally am indebted to her for many kindnesses. My warmest thanks to the members of the cast and crew, especially to the director James Kent, screenwriter Juliette Towhidi, co-producer Celia Duval, costume designer Consolata Boyle, and the actors Alicia Vikander, Kit Harington, Colin Morgan, Joanna Scanlan and Miranda Richardson. I am additionally grateful to Juliette Towhidi for allowing me to reproduce some words from her screenplay.

I am very grateful to Joe Oppenheimer for all his kindness and consideration during the six years that the film was in development, and to his colleagues at BBC Films, Christine Langan and Beth Pattinson. Thanks also to Victoria Brooks and Una Maguire at Milk Publicity, to Alice Seabright at Heyday Films, to Nick Manzi at Lionsgate and to Lennie Goodings, Publisher at Virago, who continues to keep *Testament of Youth* at the forefront of her list. I acknowledge the kind assistance of the librarians and archivists at the William Ready Special Archives at McMaster University, in Hamilton, Ontario, which houses the vast Vera Brittain Archive; and of Anne Manuel at Somerville College, Oxford, home to a smaller collection of Brittain papers amassed during the writing of the authorised biography.

Special thanks are due to Georgina Gordon-Smith at United Agents for all her expertise and supportive advice concerning the film. Thanks, too, for their consummate professionalism to my literary agents Ariella Feiner and Robert Kirby at United Agents, and to my editors at Bloomsbury, Jamie Birkett and Robin Baird-Smith.

1 Provincial Young Ladyhood
1893–1914

On 7 November 1915, Vera Brittain wrote a letter to her fiancé Roland Leighton. Roland had been out in Flanders and France for seven months, serving on the Western Front with the 7th Worcestershire Regiment. Vera had been nursing as a Voluntary Aid Detachment nurse at a military hospital in Camberwell for no more than a few weeks. She had seen him only once since his departure, when he returned home on leave in August, and they had become engaged.

Her overriding wish, she now admitted to Roland for the first time, was for an immediate end to the war. But she also wondered if war, and nursing the shattered bodies of the wounded and dying, had changed her irrevocably, and whether it was possible that she would ever be the same person again after 'some of the dreadful things I have to see here'. A week earlier, the experience of assisting at an amputation dressing had seared itself on her memory. She had come away from it 'with my hands covered in blood and my mind full of a passionate fury at the wickedness of war, and I wished that I had never been born.'

Nothing in the circumstances of Vera Brittain's background or upbringing could have prepared her for the ways in which her personal destiny would be transformed, before she had reached the age of 25, by the cataclysm of a global conflict. To Vera's generation, born in the final decade of Queen Victoria's reign, war had appeared as something remote and unimaginable: 'its monstrous destructions and distresses safely shut up', she remembered towards the end of her life, '… between the covers of history books'.

Her own future at birth had seemed comfortable, sheltered and assured. Vera Mary Brittain was born on 29 December 1893, at Atherstone House, Sidmouth Avenue, a small black and white fronted villa in Newcastle-under-Lyme, North Staffordshire. Her father was Thomas Arthur Brittain (generally known as Arthur, to distinguish him from his father and grandfather), a director of the family paper-making firm of Brittains Limited, which operated mills at Hanley in Stoke-on-Trent (one of the novelist Arnold Bennett's 'Five Towns'), and at Cheddleton, near Leek. Among the innovations at the Brittain paper mills was the development of the thin, tough and opaque paper used by Oxford University Press in the production of its prayer books and bibles.

This manufacturing success, during the last decades of the nineteenth century, had laid the foundations of the Brittain family's wealth. When old Thomas Brittain, Arthur's grandfather and the founder of the business, died in 1894, he left behind him a vast fortune of over £100,000, though money was frequently to be the

Vera Brittain at the front window of 'Melrose', her Buxton home, in about 1912.

source of bitter legal dispute among Vera's large clan of quarrelsome Brittain uncles and aunts.

In stark contrast to the Brittains' wealth, the Bervons, the family of Vera's mother Edith, came from a background of genteel poverty. Inglis Bervon, Vera's maternal grandfather, was originally from Birmingham, but had adopted a peripatetic lifestyle as a professional singer. By the time Edith, the third of six children, two boys, four girls, was born in 1868, Inglis and Emma Bervon and their family had moved to Aberystwyth where Inglis was employed as a church organist. In the mid-1880s, he set up a successful, but scarcely lucrative, practice as a singing teacher in Hanley. One of his pupils was Arthur Brittain, who was instantly attracted to Inglis's daughter, Edith.

They were married in the spring of 1891. It was not a love match, as Edith once confided to Vera, though the marriage was to last for more than 40 years and was undoubtedly a contented union for much of that time. Arthur could be irascible and, like several of his siblings, was increasingly prone to depressive illness as he got older. However, as a young man he possessed the ambition and drive of the enterprising businessman. Edith may have been socially at a disadvantage, marrying into the middle-class respectability of the Brittain family, but she dressed well, an essential prerequisite of this newfound respectability – and something in which she would be more than emulated by her daughter, who remained fashion conscious to a high degree. Furthermore Edith showed herself more than able to create a secure and tranquil home, providing a harmonious backdrop for Vera's 'serene and uneventful' childhood.

In 1895, the Brittains moved to 'Glen Bank', a large semi-detached house on the outskirts of the Cheshire silk town of Macclesfield, and it was here that Edward Harold Brittain was born, on 30 November. From an early age, an extraordinary bond existed between Vera and her brother, not quite two years her junior. It was based on their fundamentally different temperaments. She was volatile and inclined to be outspoken, characteristics belied by her outward appearance of vulnerable prettiness (an impression accentuated by her lack of height, as she grew to only five foot three inches). Edward was much calmer and more conciliatory, always ready to pour oil on troubled waters, counselling his sister to be less headstrong and confrontational in rows with their parents. In a childhood overseen by an affectionate governess but largely devoid of the company of other children, they formed a mutual dependence, broken only by their separation when they were sent away to boarding schools.

In a strangely significant parallel, one other individual was to play a comparable role in Vera Brittain's life, providing protective sympathy with at times critical, although seemingly unlimited, understanding, and that was Winifred Holtby, in the remarkable friendship that sprang up between the two women after they met each other at Somerville College, Oxford, in 1919.

But this 'serene' home background possessed one clear drawback for the young Vera Brittain. It was unbookish and unintellectual, and from an early age she began deliberately to define herself in opposition to it. Her father had attended school up to the age of 18, but had not gone on to university. Her mother's education had been minimal. Vera later bemoaned the fact that the shelves at 'Glen Bank' were home to precisely nine books, including several of Mrs Henry Wood's lachrymose romances, the complete poems of Longfellow and a copy of *Household Medicine*.

Her own identity, practically as soon as she could hold a pen, was confirmed as a literary one. As an adult she claimed never to remember a time when it wasn't her conscious intention to be a writer. Her governess constructed little notebooks out of waste-cuts brought home by Mr Brittain from the paper mill, and in these Vera wrote her five childhood 'novels'. The stories all bear the influence of Victorian melodrama, are set in or around Macclesfield and are full of violent deaths and self-sacrificing heroines (usually bearing her mother's name, Edith). Vera was a practised storyteller, regaling her brother Edward with bedtime stories centring on a mythological community known as 'The Dicks'.

Close as brother and sister were, the differences in the treatment meted out to them by their parents, and in the different expectations they had of them, must have made it obvious to Vera from childhood that a daughter would always be viewed as a second class citizen in comparison to a son. She loved Edward too dearly to resent him because of this, but the implication of female inferiority was one, nevertheless, that continued to rankle. At the beginning of her twenties, she recorded a conversation with her father in which she asked him if it wasn't equally important that she, like her brother, should have a career:

He answered very decidedly 'No, Edward was the one who must be given an occupation & the means to provide for himself.' The secondary sex again! It makes me feel angry that I, the more intellectual of the two, should be regarded in this light because I happen not to be a man. *But I will show them.* If Father though knowing me will not believe I have any value, *the belief will be forced upon him by facts.*

Vera may have been both more intelligent and more imaginative than her brother, as well as more forceful – an aspect of her character recognised by Arthur Brittain, when, in a backhanded compliment, he nicknamed her 'Jack' – but her evident precocity did not lead to the overturning of basic assumptions about her education and future. When she was sent away from home, it would be to 'good' schools that emphasised her family's social standing rather than demonstrated concerns about educational attainment. And in the longer term, as an attractive young woman from a well-off family, she would be expected to make a good marriage.

As a boy, Edward's position may have been more privileged, and his future taken more seriously, but to some extent he, too, was restricted by the constraints imposed by his gender. After public school and university, he would be expected to take the examinations for entry to the Indian Civil Service, or to start work in the family business. This would leave little room for the true passion of his life, his love of music. At school, he took up the violin and viola, as well as the piano and organ, and began to compose songs and short concertos. But music would not have been regarded by either of his parents as an appropriate occupation or future career for a 'gentleman'.

In 1905, when Vera was 11, the family left Macclesfield for the spa town of Buxton, in Derbyshire. The move signalled the Brittains' social aspirations: Buxton, with its glorious new Opera House designed by Frank Matcham, its Pavilion Gardens and its elegant eighteenth-century Crescent, had an air of wealth and refinement together with a deep vein of provincial snobbery.

Additionally, Buxton possessed a number of good day schools. Edward went to one of these in preparation for his first term at Uppingham School in Rutland, where he started as a boarder in the autumn term of 1908. Uppingham was a public school especially favoured by the families of middle-class industrialists. It was well-known for its music, but was also in the vanguard of public school militarism. There was a large and well-run Officers' Training Corps, established during the South African War, which set the tone for other school activities. No boy, for instance, was allowed to take part in a sports contest, or be awarded a school prize, without first having passed a shooting test.

In 1907, following two years at Buxton's Grange School, which described itself as 'a high-class school for the daughters of gentlemen', Vera was sent to St Monica's School in Kingswood, Surrey, where one of Edith Brittain's sisters, the eldest, Florence Bervon, was co-headmistress. Aunt Florence had been a governess to a family in Stoke before setting up St Monica's in partnership with Louise Heath-Jones, who had been an undergraduate at Newnham College, Cambridge, and a teacher at St Leonard's School in St Andrews.

St Monica's wasn't on a par with St Leonard's, nor, indeed, with still grander schools like Roedean or Benenden, and Vera only went there because of the family connection. But it was to prove a fortunate choice. Florence Bervon had neither academic qualifications nor training. She was largely responsible for administration, for teaching the girls social skills and for attracting the right kind of wealthy clientele to the school. Miss Heath-Jones, on the other hand, was much more progressive. She showed an enlightened attitude to the way certain subjects were taught, in particular history and scripture, and current events, where her pupils were given extracts from newspapers. Vera rapidly established herself at the top of the school. In her final year, lessons with a visiting mistress, Edith Fry, who encouraged her to read Carlyle, Ruskin, William Morris and modern firebrands like H. G. Wells, strengthened Vera's determination to be a writer. '[My] writing tends towards a purpose now', she recorded portentously in her diary, '– I want to write, but I will not reveal what until the time shall come'.

In a spur to Vera's developing feminism, Louise Heath-Jones introduced her to the South African feminist Olive Schreiner's pioneering work, *Woman and Labour*, not long after its publication in 1911. Schreiner's declaration of equality with men, her message to women that 'We take all labour for our province', and her accompanying plea that women be given the training 'which fits them for labour', immediately struck a chord with Vera. Furthermore, in the summer of 1911, Miss

**Vera, circa 1912, dressed in her best clothes, perhaps for one
of the Sunday Church parades in Buxton's Pavilion Gardens.**

Heath-Jones took Vera and other senior girls to a women's suffrage meeting at Tadworth. It was of the milder, constitutionalist variety, free from associations with the militant campaigns of the Pankhursts and their supporters campaigning for the vote through arson and bomb attacks on public property. Nevertheless it was a daring move on Heath-Jones's part, and one highly unlikely to have found any support from her pupils' parents.

As she approached her eighteenth birthday, in December 1911, Vera prepared to leave St Monica's and return to Buxton. Despite the ways in which she had been encouraged to think about women's rights and the possibility of a wider, independent life, her immediate prospects were inextricably linked to making a good marriage with a suitable young man. She later claimed to have been fired with an ambition to go to university from the moment she discovered 'that such places existed'. However, opportunities for higher education for women were still largely limited to those of their sex who were unlikely to marry and were therefore left to support themselves by teaching. Clearly, Vera was never going to fit into that category.

In *Woman and Labour*, Olive Schreiner had reserved some of her fiercest criticism for the parasitical dependency of middle-class women on men. 'Finely clad' and 'tenderly housed', and deprived of intelligence or vitality, 'the fine lady', or female parasite, in Schreiner's more savage term, contributes 'nothing to the active and sustaining labours of her society', and exists through the 'passive performance of sex functions only'.

It remained to be seen whether Vera would be able to find an alternative to the temptations offered by this conventional life.

At first, Vera entered enthusiastically into the world of the provincial debutante. Returning home to 'Melrose', the Brittains' large, imposing grey stone house in the select residential area of Buxton known as 'The Park', she quickly became immersed in a succession of balls and dances, 'At Homes', amateur theatricals, bridge and tennis parties, and the weekly Church Parades in the Pavilion Gardens, a prize opportunity to show off in one's Sunday best.

Vera made her debut at the High Peak Hunt Ball on 9 January 1912, in the ballroom of the Hydropathic Hotel. Newspaper reports of subsequent occasions over the course of the next two years often lavished praise on her choice of dress: for example, the 'lovely gown of canary satin charmeuse with gold and jewelled embroidery over which was most gracefully draped sky-blue ninon' she wore at the 1913 Cottage Hospital Ball.

What sort of young woman was Vera Brittain at this time? In appearance, she was attractive: small, dark-haired, with striking, deep-set hazel eyes. In personality, she could be fun-loving, though she rarely showed any evidence of a sense of humour, and could be rigorously critical of others as well as of herself. Her schooldays at St Monica's had been dominated by intense friendships with two other girls, one with Stella Sharp (who was later to nurse as a VAD with Vera in London and Malta), the other with Cora Stoop; but Vera tended to prefer the company of men.

In the autumn of 1913, as she approached her twentieth birthday, Vera received her first proposal of marriage, from a young Buxton man named Bertram Spafford, nearly a decade older than she was, whom she subsequently condemned for his 'limited brains and evangelical principles'. 'My dear Vera', he wrote, 'The night I took you down to dinner at your house 16 months ago, I first knew I loved you – and since then you have been everything in the whole world to me ... Is there the faintest chance of you caring for me even a little – and will you give me a chance of winning you ... [?]'. Her response was terse, and exhibited a note of contempt. She had been 'very sorry' to receive his letter. 'I cannot for a moment entertain the idea of your proposal, and I must beg you to consider this as final, as I have no doubt whatsoever of my feelings on the subject'.

Even so, she did not completely discourage Spafford. She hung alluringly over the gate at 'Melrose' if she saw him in the vicinity of The Park, and continued to behave flirtatiously whenever they met. 'To fall in love with him would be a perfect impossibility, but it is very easy to fall in love with love', she admitted in her diary. 'To hear a man's voice say "you" in a tone which he uses to no one else on earth, is in itself a gigantic temptation to make him go on saying it like that ... It is wrong ... but then I am not good, & in spite of high purposes, only a very human girl'.

Vera's diary, which she had begun at school in 1910, had by now evolved into a more earnest 'Reflective Record'. In it she reasserted her intention of becoming a writer and of recording 'all the things, absurd, pathetic, interesting, original, humorous, satirical, that strike me as being useful for material'. The diary proved an outlet for her growing hatred of Buxton itself, which came to epitomise to Vera the mean, fault-finding spirit of the provincial town: inward-looking and narrowly class-regimented, in which everyone knew everyone else's business and was unable to resist passing comment on it. She described her clashes with her father, who continued to ridicule her feminist beliefs, and portrayed her closeness to her mother – often united with Vera against the patriarch in the house – to an extent that will surprise readers of her later accounts, in which Edith Brittain is a more distant and sometimes less sympathetic or supportive figure.

Throughout 1913 and 1914, Vera also used her diary to express her longing for a more meaningful existence, beyond the social whirl of parties and dances and other trivial pursuits. In some entries, the frivolous side of her character competes openly with the desire to be more serious and idealistic. She delighted in an afternoon's bridge party with some neighbours, in February 1913, but then returned home to finish reading George Eliot's *Felix Holt*, which filled her with a desire to imitate the young radical Holt by holding up 'an ideal for humanity'. Vera bolstered her confidence with declarations of her own superiority – her determination to be an 'exceptional & brilliant person', for example, or her recognition that 'I always come out top in the end, & I always shall' – that need to be understood in the context of a home life in which her hopes and aspirations often failed to be taken seriously. And she wrote of her loneliness, in the absence of any companion of her own age and with Edward still at Uppingham during term time. This in turn increased her resolve to be more independent, and to 'stand alone'.

One drama that bulked large in her diary in 1913-14 – and was to provide the raw material, a decade later, for the least successful of Vera's five published novels, *Not Without Honour* – was the controversy that had erupted over the views of a local rationalist clergyman, Joseph Ward. Ward was the young Anglican curate of St Peter's Church, at Fairfield, a neighbouring village to Buxton. Vera had read *Robert Elsmere*, Mrs Humphry Ward's late nineteenth century novel about a clergyman who rejects superstition and dogma in order to pursue a life of service among the poor in the East End of London; and Ward, who preached the social relevance of Christ's teaching while rejecting traditional theology, appeared to her like a real-life Elsmere.

In a sense the storm stirred up by Ward, who was denounced as subversive by his social betters – including Arthur Brittain – but looked upon as a spiritual leader by the poor of Fairfield, belonged to a bygone age. To Vera, however, the controversy reflected her own spiritual doubts about Christ's divinity and the relevance of orthodox Christian doctrine, and she regularly walked the three miles to Fairfield for Ward's services, sometimes in the company of her mother or Edward.

The extent of her fascination and, at times, of her infatuation with Ward comes across clearly in diary entries. What additionally made Ward a significant influence on her was his support for Vera's decision to attempt to win a place at Oxford University. She had

Vera in 1913, at about the time she started studying for Oxford University. 'Oxford I trust may lead to something', she wrote, 'but Buxton never will.'

begun to see college as perhaps the only means, outside marriage, of escaping from Buxton, though she worried initially that academia might prevent her from reaching her ultimate goal of becoming a writer.

Vera's attendance together with her mother at a series of Oxford University Extension lectures, given by John Marriott at Buxton's Town Hall in early 1913, encouraged her to take the idea of higher education seriously for the first time.* The award of a prize for one of her essays, and her visit to Oxford that August, chaperoned by Aunt Florence and Miss Heath-Jones, to take part in the summer meeting of the University Extension Delegacy, finally led her to make a firm decision in Oxford's favour and to start enquiring about a choice of college.

She also managed to overcome any resistance from her father to paying the fees, and to funding the cost of the tuition necessary for the entrance exam. Indeed, if anyone had doubts about Vera's course of action at this stage, it was not her parents but Vera herself, worrying about how easily Oxford women students could be identified with dowdy, spinsterish school teachers forced to earn their own living.

Vera decided to try for Somerville College. Founded in 1879, Somerville, with its 150 students and dozen or so dons, possessed the highest intellectual standards of the four women's colleges. A preliminary interview with

---

* The extension movement, established in the final decades of the nineteenth century, was designed to promote the spread of learning beyond the universities. Women, permitted to study at university, but still prevented from taking degrees, were one of its main audiences.

the college's Principal, Emily Penrose, to some extent confirmed Vera's fears about academic dowdiness, when Miss Penrose widened her eyes in disapproval at Vera's inappropriately 'gay attire', and in consequent 'disbelief' at her intellect. Vera was advised to read English, and on no account to try for the scholarship. However, after consulting Edward, who would himself before long win a place at New College for the Michaelmas Term of 1914, Vera decided to sit the scholarship anyway.

In another complicated hurdle, she would in any case have to sit two exams: the college scholarship in March 1914, and the Oxford Senior Local for university entry that July. Setting to work, she studied intensively, working by herself, and in private lessons with the local crammer Mr Lace, taking time off only for a game of tennis or golf. Remarking on Buxton's collective amazement at her decision to go to college, Vera observed that 'In a small narrow place like this, one half thinks me too go-ahead for words, & the other absolutely mad & a perfect fool'.

On the first day of the exam at Somerville, however, she quickly discovered that she had been studying along the wrong lines, reading too much criticism of the writers rather than the writers themselves. Beginning the first paper, she almost lost her nerve and thought of packing up and going home. But she regained her composure and decided that she had nothing to lose by staying and completing the exam.

Vera's persistence was rewarded a few days later when a letter arrived from Miss Penrose informing her that the College had awarded her an exhibition (a minor scholarship) of £20 per annum – roughly £2000 in modern terms – for three years, on condition that she passed the Oxford Senior Local in July.

Her parents were overcome with pride and delight, and for Vera a new chapter seemed to beckon. 'Oxford I trust may lead to something', she wrote, drawing a line under this period of her life, 'but Buxton never will'.

At this point, Roland Leighton enters the story properly for the first time.* In mid-April, a month after the Somerville exam, Roland arrived at Melrose to spend part of the Easter holidays with his school friend Edward Brittain. At least, that was originally the plan, but in the course of the visit he found himself more often than not in the company of Edward's sister, discussing their ideas of immortality, talking about books, criticising each other's poetry – and succumbing to a mutual attraction. At just 19, Roland was the golden boy of his year at Uppingham School. He was head of his (and Edward's) house, The Lodge; a Praepositor (school prefect); President of the Debating Society; Editor of the school magazine. His outstanding academic record at the school had been crowned at the beginning of the year with the award of the Senior Open Classical Postmastership at Merton College, Oxford, for the coming October. Together with Edward, and another friend from their house, Victor Richardson, Roland formed part of an inseparable trio,

---

* Vera had first met Roland the previous June at the Uppingham 'Old Boys'. In her diary she recorded that 'he seems so clever & amusing & hardly shy at all.'

dubbed by his mother 'The Three Musketeers'. He was the undoubted leader of this small group, as his school nickname, 'Monseigneur', testified.

Although Roland was her junior by more than a year, Vera was never to think of him as younger for, as she wrote later, he looked 24, and had the self-assurance and confidence of someone of 30. He was disdainful of popularity (another thing they had in common), conceited, and inclined to express his condescending response to other people's ideas in what she mockingly referred to as 'the Quiet Voice'. In looks he was less striking, of stocky build and with 'hair like a brush & a mouth too resolute for the smallest degree of beauty'. He did, however, have 'deep intelligent eyes', and was indisputably brilliant, '& most interesting to talk to'.

Crucially, there was something else about Roland that made him stand out for Vera: both his parents were writers, and he, too, had clear ambitions in this direction, publishing his poetry in the Uppingham magazine, and allowing Edward to set one of his poems, entitled 'L'Envoi', to music. Robert Leighton, Roland's father, had in 1896 been the first literary editor of Northcliffe's *Daily Mail*, and was the author of adventure stories for boys. His mother, Marie Connor Leighton, daughter of a captain in the 87th Royal Irish Foot, wrote popular romances, serialised in the Northcliffe Press, and collaborated on works of detective fiction with her husband. Marie's own books, though, were the Leighton family's main source of income. The early realisation that the entire household revolved around his mother's writing, as his father's earned much less, Roland claimed, had made him a feminist.

Not that feminism found any favour in Marie Leighton's eyes. She liked tidy, conventional, romantic endings, and said that she would have been happy to be a kept woman if only her husband's income had permitted. Marie was the archetypal romantic novelist. Eccentric, and larger than life, she was usually resplendent in enormous hats and colourful, unfashionable clothes, generally trailing petticoats. The Leightons with their three children – a daughter, Clare, and younger son, Evelyn, completed the family – led a chaotic, bohemian existence at 'Vallombrosa', their exotically named London home at 40 Abbey Road, St John's Wood, where they socialised with famous writers like George Meredith and Hall Caine, struggled to meet deadlines and avoided their creditors (only the lower classes, Marie maintained, paid their bills on time). Every summer the family, their servants and dogs, migrated to a turreted seaside villa at Lowestoft in Suffolk, perched perilously high on top of a cliff.

The household may have revolved around Marie's work, but her passion and devotion centred on Roland to the exclusion of everyone else. Marie's love for him was an extraordinary fixation, deriving no doubt from the death of her first child, another son, accidentally smothered by his nurse soon after his birth. As an infant, Roland was spoiled by a mother who dressed him in expensive clothes and refused to allow his long blonde curls to be cut. Marie and Roland shared their own special intimacy, which naturally contributed to his sense of himself as far above the ordinary, while relegating his younger sister and brother to an upbringing of casual emotional neglect.

Before Vera departed Buxton to visit some relatives in the Lake District, leaving Roland behind at Melrose to make up for lost time with Edward, Roland made a promise that he would send her a copy of his favourite book, a novel by Olive Schreiner entitled *The Story of an African Farm*. A copy duly arrived, inscribed by Roland, with a letter in which he wrote of Vera's resemblance to Lyndall, the novel's feminist heroine, who defies convention, but then has the misfortune to die in the process as the result of giving birth to a child out of wedlock; only Roland considered Lyndall 'sadder & less charmingly controversial'.

Like Lyndall, Vera confided to her diary, one May evening, that she desired not only sympathetic companionship but also 'someone to worship'. But who was the object of that worship to be? Joseph Ward, the Fairfield curate, whose struggles, in between further Latin and Maths for her Oxford exam, Vera was still following closely, or Roland Leighton?

Three days at Uppingham, accompanied by Mrs Brittain, for Edward's final Speech Day in the second week of July, the high point of the school year, confirmed Roland's attraction for her. He shared her faults, talents and ideas, Vera told her diary, to a degree she hadn't experienced before. Not only did he play a leading part in the inspection of the Officers Training Corps, in which he held the rank of Colour Sergeant, he also carried off an unprecedented seven prizes at the prize-giving. At the Headmaster's garden party that followed, she and Roland got into an earnest discussion about *The Story of an African Farm*, and Roland's conviction that there must

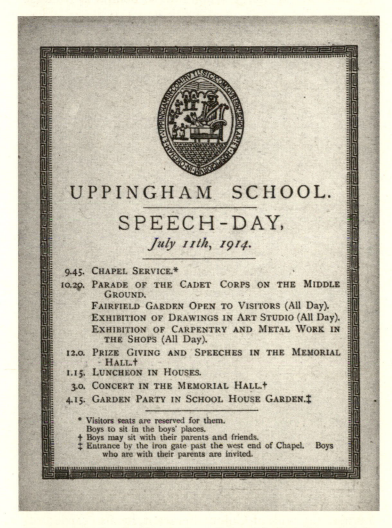

UPPINGHAM SCHOOL.

SPEECH-DAY,

July 11th, 1914.

9.45. CHAPEL SERVICE.*
10.20. PARADE OF THE CADET CORPS ON THE MIDDLE GROUND.
   FAIRFIELD GARDEN OPEN TO VISITORS (All Day).
   EXHIBITION OF DRAWINGS IN ART STUDIO (All Day).
   EXHIBITION OF CARPENTRY AND METAL WORK IN THE SHOPS (All Day).
12.0. PRIZE GIVING AND SPEECHES IN THE MEMORIAL HALL.†
1.15. LUNCHEON IN HOUSES.
3.0. CONCERT IN THE MEMORIAL HALL.†
4.15. GARDEN PARTY IN SCHOOL HOUSE GARDEN.‡

   * Visitors seats are reserved for them.
     Boys to sit in the boys' places.
   † Boys may sit with their parents and friends.
   ‡ Entrance by the iron gate past the west end of Chapel. Boys
     who are with their parents are invited.

Programme for the Uppingham School Speech Day, in July 1914, later described by Vera as 'the one perfect summer idyll that I ever experienced'.

be an after-life in which human beings could continue the work that they had begun on earth. Vera's only regret about her time at Uppingham was that she had been unable to meet Roland's mother, reportedly detained at home finishing a book.

Edward and Victor Richardson, the other two 'musketeers', looked upon Roland with awe, even as they fought to escape from his shadow and teased him about his conceit. Edward, who played a violin solo in the school concert, had failed to come out top in any subject. It was his 'special prerogative', he told his mother, disappointedly, to be second or third in everything he did. Victor Richardson had won prizes for Modern History and reading, and was destined for Emmanuel College, Cambridge, where he had a place to read medicine. The son of the junior partner of a dental practice from Hove, in East Sussex, Victor was recovering from the family tragedy that had deprived him, and his younger brother Maurice, of their mother, 18 months earlier. Carrie Richardson had been 47 at the time of her death from cerebrospinal meningitis. As his nicknames, 'Father Confessor' and 'The Brighton Block', suggest, Victor was a loyal and steadfast friend, valued for his discretion with other people's confidences (indicating, perhaps, that he may already have had the makings of a good bedside-manner).

At the prize-giving ceremony, on 11 July, the Headmaster, the Revd H. W. McKenzie, gave a short speech, the climax of which was that 'if a man could not be useful to his country he was better dead'. Vera copied the remark into her diary without comment.

Uppingham's ethos of militarism – and its related values of honour, chivalry, duty and 'heroism in the abstract' – was preparing pupils for the eventuality of a war in which public schoolboys like Roland, Edward and Victor would play a leading part. Vera's own attraction to these ideals was evident. She admired the 'fine sight' of the Corps, as it was inspected by the Headmaster, listened attentively to his speech, describing him as 'a splendid man' – in spite of 'his contempt for women' – and regretted the absence of an equivalent to Uppingham's 'fine traditions' at schools for girls.

In fact war clouds were beginning to gather much more threateningly than anyone at Uppingham, during three fine days of glorious, unbroken weather, could have suspected. On 20 July, Vera sat the exam for the Oxford Senior Local Examinations. A fortnight later the international situation reached a crisis point when Germany invaded Belgium as a preliminary to an attack on France. At 11 p.m., on 4 August 1914, Britain declared war on Germany.

2 Love and War 1914–1915

Although she would later try to distance herself from them, Vera Brittain's views and opinions in August 1914, as expressed in her diary and letters, demonstrate a predominantly conventional response to the outbreak of war. She had followed closely the build-up to the July Crisis, and the resulting 'world-wide catastrophe', with mounting excitement. On 25 July she recorded Austria's ultimatum to Serbia and, four days later, the declaration of war between the two countries, which lit the touch paper for a conflagration that would set Europe ablaze. By Saturday 1 August, following news of the mobilisation of the German army, Vera realised that the last hopes for peace were rapidly receding. On the third, after reading various newspapers for a couple of hours over breakfast, she announced to her diary: 'That which has been so long anticipated by some & scoffed at by others has come to pass at last – Armageddon in Europe!'

Britain alone appeared to tremble on the brink, with Asquith's Liberal cabinet split on the momentous question of whether to enter the war to come to France's aid. At this point, Vera's diary entries swell with all the bombastic rhetoric of a leader from *The Times*. 'The great fear now', she wrote on Bank Holiday Monday, 3 August, the day on which the Foreign Secretary Sir Edward Grey appealed in the House of Commons for the country's support for war, 'is that our bungling Government will declare England's neutrality'. Adopting Grey's line, Vera argued that it would be an act of 'the grossest treachery' should 'we at this critical juncture ... refuse to help our friend France.'

Accompanied by her parents the next day, Vera rushed into the centre of town to search for further news. A large crowd surrounded the front of Buxton's Town Hall, where a mobilisation order in eye-catching black letters had been posted, ordering army regulars and territorials to their headquarters. Germany's invasion of Belgium had satisfied most of the waverers in the Government by giving Britain's cause a moral rectitude, and the evening paper contained the startling news that Britain had sent an ultimatum to Germany, to expire at 11 p.m. (Greenwich Mean Time), demanding the immediate withdrawal of her troops from Belgium. Vera imagined 'All the nations of this continent ... ready with their swords drawn', while 'Germany the aggressor with her weaker ally Austria stands alone facing an armed Europe united against her'. But she also recognised that this would be a mechanised war like no other in history, and that 'the destruction attainable by the modern war machines used by the armies is unthinkable & past imagination.'

On 5 August, in the absence of any response to its ultimatum, the country awoke to find itself at war with Germany. Later that day, Vera showed Edward an appeal, printed in *The Times* and the *Chronicle*, for unmarried men between the ages of 18 and 30 to join the army. He immediately became very enthusiastic about volunteering, and set about trying to offer himself as a recruit, along with his school friend and Buxton neighbour Maurice Ellinger, initially without much success.

Vera's eagerness to support her brother's desire to enlist was matched only by her father's obduracy in opposing it. As Edward, at 18, was below military age, he required his father's permission before his application could be accepted by the War Office, and this Arthur Brittain stubbornly withheld, much to Vera's indignation. '… Daddy worked himself into a thorough temper, raved away at us, & said he would not allow Edward to go abroad whatever happened … Edward replied quite calmly that no one could prevent him serving his country in any way he wanted to.'

The extent of Vera's investment in the public school values of duty, honour and heroism, and in a conventional ideal of middle-class masculinity, was to become even clearer as the family continued to debate Edward's future. She reproached her father for his 'unmanliness', and for not possessing 'the requisite courage'. She worried that other Buxtonians might judge them unfavourably. Most of all, she subscribed to Edward's somewhat priggish belief that Mr Brittain's lack of a public school education and training meant that he 'could not possibly understand the impossibility of his remaining in inglorious safety while others, scarcely older than he, were offering their all.' Mr Brittain, Vera wrote scathingly in her diary, after the row had raged for a month, did not care about

flights trying to get along the railways, particularly
back to England. Paper money is useless & the
majority of the trains are cut off. None of them
are allowed to cross the frontier, & tourists
besides travelling fifteen in a carriage intended
for six have to get out at the frontiers &
take their own luggage across. Nancy Jarrett
does not know what will become of her German
cousins who tried to return to Berlin on Friday.
It is rumoured that there is fear in Paris that
a fleet of German Zeppelins are going to destroy
Paris from above in the night. Truly it is a
situation never equalled & scarcely imagined
within the memory of living men.

Tuesday August 4th.

Late as it is & almost too excited to write as I
am I must make some effort to chronicle
the stupendous events of this remarkable day.
The situation is absolutely unparalleled in the
history of the world. Never before has the war
strength of each individual nation been of such

Vera's diary entry for 4 August 1914, expressing her excitement at 'the stupendous events of this remarkable day' as
Britain moved inexorably closer to war.

great extent, even though of all the nations of Europe the dominant continent, have been all armed before. It is estimated that when the war begins 14 millions of men will be engaged in the conflict. Attack is possible by earth, water & air, & the destruction attainable by the modern war machines used by the armies is unthinkable & past imagination.

This morning at breakfast we learnt that war is formally declared between France & Germany that the German ambassador has left Paris & the French ambassador Berlin. Germany has declared to Belgium that if her troops are allowed to pass unmolested through Belgian territory she will protect her interests in the treaty at the end of the war. Belgium has indignantly refused any such violation of her national honour, and the King of the Belgians has appealed to King George for aid. For an hour this morning I read a fine speech of Sir Edward Grey's, in which he manages successfully to steer the middle course his son's honour or courage as long as he was safe. She and Edward would have to live up to their patriotic name of 'Brittain' as their father manifestly would not.

Ultimately, Arthur Brittain was forced to give way, especially after Edith Brittain, who had initially expressed similar reservations about Edward entering the army, conceded that if Edward's honour was at stake then he really should be permitted to go. '... Dreary as life is without his presence here,' Vera had admitted from the outset, 'dreary as are the prospects of what may lie before him, yet I would not have his decision back, or keep him here'. Later, seeing Edward in his uniform, she imbued him with martial glamour and judged him 'a fit object of devotion'.

By understanding how important it was that her brother should not be 'branded for life' because he had failed to take part 'in the greatest struggle in modern times', Vera was implicitly acknowledging the already widespread existence of white feather campaigns, spearheaded by women and currently springing up around the country. Women's handing out of white feathers – a traditional symbol of cowardice – was a deliberate act of public humiliation to shame men not in uniform into enlisting.

The impact of these campaigns, coupled with the effects of government propaganda encouraging women to play a part in pressuring men to volunteer, can be seen in Vera's reaction to her erstwhile suitor, Bertram Spafford. Spafford at first resisted applying for a commission, as he was concerned about the effect that enlisting might have upon his business. Vera directly attributed his lack of response to the call of King and Country to the fact that he had been educated at Manchester Grammar School, which, unlike Uppingham, had no Officers Training Corps. One day in early September, she observed Spafford pushing his mother in a bath chair through Buxton's Pavilion Gardens. Contemplating 'his obvious strength and suitability for military work', she branded him 'a shirker', in the pages of her diary.

Recounting to Roland Leighton the 'domestic storms' that it had been necessary to live through before Edward was allowed to enlist, Vera wrote that she had 'persistently urged from the beginning of the war that Edward ought at least to try for something'. Not, she quickly added, that she was 'in the slightest degree a militarist':

> But it seems to me that to refrain from fighting in a cause like this because you do not approve of warfare would be about as sensible as refusing to defend yourself against the attacks of a madman because you did not consider lunacy an enlightened or desirable condition.

What Vera appears to be saying here is that, while she opposes war in general, she sees the European war of 1914, with its threat of a German aggressor seeking hegemony over the entire continent, as a particular case, necessitating special action.

Three weeks into the war, at the end of August, Vera learned at last that she had reached the required standard in the Oxford Senior Local Examination, and that her exhibition at Somerville was consequently secure. Her pleasure at the news was immediately spoiled by her father's reaction. It was no use her thinking of going to Oxford with a war on, he told her angrily, though Mr Brittain quickly appears to have reversed this decision, leaving Vera to tell Roland that he could hope to see her at Oxford that October.

'You *will* go, won't you?', she asked him. It wasn't simply the war that might stand in his way but also the family finances, which, as so often, were in a fairly precarious state. However, on 28 August Roland wrote to say that, with the help of a school-leaving exhibition of £30 a year, 'I think I shall be able to manage it all right', and that he looked forward to the three of them – Vera, Edward and himself – being together at Oxford.

That dream soon faded. A month later, with the start of the academic year just ten days away, a letter from Roland admitted that he was no longer certain that he would be coming to Oxford. He had hopes, like Edward, and like Victor Richardson, their Uppingham friend, 'of doing something of what now alone really counts'. A commission as a second lieutenant in the 4th Norfolks, despite his poor eyesight, now seemed a distinct possibility.

He would miss the 'incidental pleasure' of seeing Vera at university, but in the circumstances it would be impossible to endure a life of what he called 'scholastic vegetation'. It would seem 'a somewhat cowardly shirking' – that heavily loaded word again – of his duty.

He felt that he was intended for an active part in the war. In its next few lines, his letter reveals the strongest influence of the Uppingham ethos. To Roland, war was 'a very fascinating thing – something, if often horrible, yet very ennobling and very beautiful, something whose elemental reality raises it above the reach of all cold theorising'.

Rather than make the slightest criticism of his change of plans, Vera's response emphasised that Roland was making the right choice. She found something ennobling in war too, she told him, and was in no doubt that had she been a boy she would long since have gone off to take part in it. 'Women get all the dreariness of war & none of its exhilaration', she exclaimed, with a driving sense of frustration; and in the coming months she was often to experience the war vicariously through the lives of her brother and her male friends. For the time being, though, she had already begun the only war work that 'it seems possible as yet for women to do': knitting bed-socks and sleeping-helmets for soldiers, attending bandaging classes, and sitting a First Aid exam with other Buxton ladies.

Edward, as it turned out, would be at Oxford that autumn, not at New College, but training with the University's OTC, and Vera hoped to see something of him while he was there. In November, he would be gazetted as a Second Lieutenant in the 11th Sherwood Foresters and sent to Frensham, in Surrey. It would be the beginning of a long period of home service with no indication of when he might be transferred to the Western Front. Roland meanwhile was billeted in Norwich as a subaltern with the 4th Norfolks, responsible for the battalion signalling section and despatch riders.

Roland's decision to forego Oxford, perhaps indefinitely, had tarnished Vera's hopes of getting to know him gradually, as well as planting the first seeds of doubt in her mind regarding the relevance of the intellectual, or 'contemplative', life to the concerns of the wider world in wartime. Nevertheless the excitement she felt at her new, independent existence at Somerville, which began on 9 October, quickly succeeded in pushing the war into the background, and before long she had ceased to follow current events as closely in newspapers. And despite the exchange of several letters with him, Vera's immersion in Oxford also reduced for the time being the significance of Roland Leighton as a focus in her life.

Not that she cared in the slightest degree for the exclusively female community represented by Somerville. It was the kind of lifestyle that was always anathema to her, and the wartime departure of so many male dons and undergraduates into the army had given the University a novel feminine atmosphere. While noting that she appeared to have picked up her customary reputation for being earnest and conceited – in addition to one for being 'the lion' of her year – Vera recorded in her diary the beginnings of several new friendships. One was with Norah Hughes, from Winchester, whose experiences with 'the Cathedral set' of hating dances and being thought mad to want to go to university mirrored Vera's own. Another, more competitive, relationship was with Una Ellis-Fermor, a London girl, later a distinguished scholar of Elizabethan drama. Liberated from her restrictive life at home, Vera revelled in cocoa evenings, with their animated discussions of dons and third years, trips to the theatre – 'on the cheap, which is half the joy' – and singing in the University's Bach Choir alongside Dorothy L. Sayers, the future crime novelist and a fellow Somervillian.

She was having to work very hard. Vera had been accepted to read English, but in order to be eligible for the B.A. degree – if and when the university granted degrees for women – she had to prepare for two exams in her first year: Responsions Greek that December, and Pass Moderations, comprising papers in mathematics as well as Classics, the following summer. In Greek, which Vera was learning from scratch with extra coaching, Vera's determination was strengthened by her desire to impress the Classics tutor, Hilda Lorimer. This was not easily achieved. Miss Lorimer, with her harsh Scottish accent, acerbic manner and deep knowledge of Homer, was scornful of Vera's best efforts. But by the end of term, when the Greek coach Mr May gave Vera an outstanding report, Miss Lorimer's attitude towards her had begun to change.

Vera sat her exam in Oxford's Sheldonian Theatre on 9 December, before returning to Buxton for Christmas. Three days later, a telegram informed her that she had passed Responsions Greek (the fact that she had done so on six week's acquaintance with the language, she admitted later, testified to the 'simplicity' of Responsions as an examination).

With studying out of the way for the holidays, Vera's thoughts centred once more on Roland. Determined to get to the Front as quickly as possible, Roland was in Aldershot seeking a transfer to another battalion, unsuccessfully as it transpired, which was due to leave for France in a matter of weeks. He was suffering from 'mental starvation', and longing for half-an-hour's talk 'with someone with some personality and temperament.' In her next letter, Vera enclosed a pair of bed-socks which she had knitted for him as a defence against the winter cold. They agreed to exchange photographs: Roland was worried that his might be spoilt by the incipient moustache he was growing. Vera would turn 21 at the end of that month, and he asked to be allowed to give her a present for her birthday. '... I simply *cannot* deny myself the joy of receiving a book both from him & inscribed by him', Vera confided to her diary. 'For the present I am bound to leave the feeling at that & not analyse it further lest I should discover too much. He interests me so deeply & so strangely this serious-minded, brilliant, unusual young man ...'.

Three days after Christmas, Vera received a letter from Roland suggesting that they meet in London at the end of the month. Mrs Leighton had taken a flat near Regent's Park for the purpose of interviewing her publisher. The idea of at last meeting 'Marie Connor Leighton, the authoress of sensational novels', intrigued Vera almost as much as she was attracted by the prospect of seeing Roland again, though she worried that, as an Oxford woman student, she might suggest to Mrs Leighton someone dowdy and uninteresting, like 'a pupil teacher or under-secretary for research in Church History'.

Mrs Brittain's younger, unmarried, sister, Belle, was conveniently available to chaperone her niece during two

The photograph of herself that Vera sent to Roland Leighton in December 1914. Later, three snapshots would be taken of Vera with Roland. But although these were returned to his family after Roland's death, they appear not to have survived.

days in London. Fortunately for Vera, Aunt Belle was more of a fun-loving and happy-go-lucky character than her starchier sisters, Florence and Edith. Furthermore, Belle thoroughly relished the hint of romantic assignation surrounding the occasion. On 30 December, the two women, accompanied by Edward, who was re-joining his battalion, took the train to London.

It was five months since Vera and Roland had met. He was dressed in khaki, which, however, seemed 'perfectly natural', as this was how she remembered him from the last occasion they had seen each other, during the Corps review at the Uppingham Speech Day. Throughout lunch at the Comedy Restaurant they both remained tongue-tied. Later, as they walked down darkened Regent's Street, the street lights extinguished for fear of Zeppelin raids, and with Aunt Belle and Edward hurrying along in front to give them time alone, Vera found herself wondering exactly what she did feel for Roland.

He had told her that he wanted to get to the Front as soon as possible, and Aunt Belle had helpfully reminded Vera that in these wartime circumstances this might well be their final meeting. 'In this time of tragedy there can be no postponement', Vera wrote, echoing those sentiments in her diary that evening. After a sleepless night, kept awake by thoughts of Roland, she was reunited with him the next day, New Year's Eve. At the Criterion in Piccadilly that afternoon, Vera was introduced to Mrs Leighton, and to Roland's 16-year-old sister, Clare. In spite of all Vera's trepidation beforehand about what Marie Leighton might think of her, the two women instantly established a rapport. 'She's quite human after all', Mrs Leighton exclaimed. 'I thought she might be very academic & learned'.

Alone again – with Aunt Belle – they dined at the Florence Restaurant, where Vera faced Roland with a direct question: would he like to be killed in action? He answered 'quite quietly':

Yes, I should; I don't want to die, but if I must, I should like to die that way. Anyhow, I should hate to go right through this war without being wounded at all; I should want something to prove that I had been in action.

In the course of dinner, she thought she saw him looking at her with a look that was close to undisguised admiration. For her part, during a performance of Herbert Tree's production of *David Copperfield* at His Majesty's Theatre, for which Roland, at her request, had obtained tickets, Vera found herself concentrating less and less on the play and increasingly on Roland's physical closeness to her. 'Almost everything we could have said to each other had been left unsaid', she remarked, writing up the evening in her diary. But she was certain now that the feelings that had always seemed possible ever since she had known him were now a reality, and that she was in love with Roland Leighton.

The year 1915, with all its potential for grief as well as joy, came in as Vera sat in the train back to Buxton, watching the dim lights of the railway go by in the blurred mist. The realisation of first love was suddenly diminishing

Vera's feminist beliefs and desire for independence, and she wrote in her diary that she would willingly sacrifice her hopes for a life of glittering achievement in order one day to be the mother of Roland's child.

On her way back to Oxford for the new term, Vera managed to meet Roland again, this time out of the gaze of parents or chaperone. Roland, who was now stationed at Peterborough, suggested that they meet at Leicester where she could change trains to Oxford. Inventing an excuse for her parents' benefit about not taking the usual route via Birmingham, Vera spent a couple of hours with Roland in Leicester. After lunch he insisted on continuing the journey with her all the way to Oxford. As the city came into view, the train slowed down and she stood up to put out her hand to say goodbye. Roland suddenly raised it to his lips and kissed it. 'Taken by surprise I resisted a little but quite unavailingly in his strong grip, & after all I did not really want to resist.'

The war, and the likelihood of Roland's departure for the front, was accelerating the pace of Vera's and Roland's relationship. The confirmation of her feelings for him was also in its turn slowly altering her attitude to the prospect of remaining as an undergraduate during wartime. Back at Somerville, Vera received warm congratulations on her exam performance, but 'the contemplative life', as Roland had slightingly referred to it, was beginning to seem increasingly an irrelevance.

What began to push her in the direction of a new course of action was the sudden news, in the middle of March, that Roland had achieved a transfer to a

Territorial regiment, the 7th Worcesters, which would shortly be leaving for France. There was only enough time for a hastily arranged farewell for Vera and Roland at Buxton.

She recognised that the moment had arrived which would end all hope of any peace of mind for her until the war was over. In an emotional and fragmentary conversation at 'Melrose', with both of them lapsing into long silences from time to time, Vera told Roland of her conviction that either he or Edward – but only one of them – would return from the war, and that consequently she must live with the 'Shadow of Death' hanging over her, darkening her future. They spoke of marriage and Vera mentioned her mother's fear that she would end up an intellectual old maid, and that that was indeed what she would probably become. 'I don't see why', he said. 'Simply because there will be no one left for me to marry after the war', she replied. 'Not even me?', he asked. Taking her hand, Roland kissed it as he had in the train at Oxford – 'but this time there was no glove upon it.'

On the morning of 19 March, in the first of many wartime railway station partings, Vera saw Roland off at Buxton station on his way back to Maldon, in Essex, to re-join his battalion. 'I did not wish him glory or honour or triumph; in comparison with seeing him again I cared about none of these things. So all I could say was just "I hope Heaven will be kind to me & bring you back."' Late at night, on 31 March, Roland and his battalion reached Boulogne from Folkestone, on board the *SS Onward*. A little over a week later, they arrived at Armentières, a town on the Franco–Belgian border, and, on the evening of 11 April, Roland prepared to take his platoon into the trenches for the first time. 'I wonder if I shall be afraid when I first get under fire', he wrote to Vera in a letter that he signed off with the words, 'Best of love'.

The 'Reflective Record', begun by Vera in what must now have seemed like the far off days of provincial young ladyhood, was turning into something closer to 'an autobiographical novel', as she copied into it long excerpts from Roland's letters, used the diary as a confessional for her feelings for him, and conveyed her anguished speculation when his letters failed to arrive leaving her to imagine that there had been time for him to be killed a hundred times over. Within a few weeks of Roland's departure, she was already writing of her feeling that she was writing a novel 'about someone else & not myself at all', investing Roland with something of the 'intangibility' of her imagination. In Turgenev's *On the Eve*, one of the books that Roland had given her for her 21st birthday, she found that the love scenes between Elena and Dmitri drove her 'wild with desire' for him, and demonstrated what they might be 'capable of rising to' when they were in each other's company again.

The limited opportunities that had existed for the couple to meet since falling in love encouraged the creation of this romantic narrative during their long months of separation. In their letters, too, Vera and Roland were able to be more open to each other about their feelings, in contrast to the shyness and reserve that predominated when they met face to face. In one early letter, Roland told Vera that he had been kissing her photograph. She understood that it was 'the nearness of death which breaks down the reserves & conventions', while admitting that she envied the photograph: 'it is more fortunate than its original'. Roland's response left her in no doubt of his intention on his return: 'When it is all finished and I am with her again the original shall not envy the photograph.'

His letters did not disguise from her the grim reality of trench warfare. Nothing in the newspapers, she told him, 'not the most vivid and heart-rending descriptions have made me realise war like your letters.' Roland's graphic descriptions of the trenches themselves, 'honey-combed' like a small town with passages and dug-outs (or 'bug-hutches' as they were known), gave her a clear picture of his new surroundings; while the 'crooning whistle' of shells flying overhead, creating a massive circular depression 'like a pudding basin' when they fell, told her something of the imminent danger he faced with each fresh round of duty.

Nor did he attempt to hide the more gruesome sights from her. At Ploegsteert Wood ('Plug Street Wood' as British troops christened it), part of the Ypres Salient, where Roland's battalion took over a line of trenches at the beginning of the third week of April, the German soldiers were so close – no more than sixty yards away – that, going out at night into no man's land, Roland could hear their voices. One morning he discovered the dead body of a British soldier, hidden in the undergrowth, apparently killed in the early part of the war during fierce fighting in the wood. 'The ground was slightly marshy', Roland reported to Vera, 'and the body had sunk down into it so that only the toes of his boots stuck up above the soil. His cap and equipment were just by the side, half-buried and rotting away. I am having a mound of earth thrown over him, to add one more to the little graves in the wood.'

The experience of coming upon the body was the inspiration for Roland's poem – almost certainly his first since arriving at the Front – the 'Villanelle', 'Violets from Plug Street Wood', completed on 25 April. He picked four violets, growing on the roof of his dug-out, and enclosed them in a letter to Vera. He had intended to send the poem with them, but kept it back for revision, only giving it to Vera some months later.

> Violets from Plug Street Wood,
> Sweet, I send you oversea.
> (It is strange they should be blue,
> Blue, when his soaked blood was red,
> For they grew around his head;
> It is strange they should be blue.)

> Violets from Plug Street Wood-
> Think what they have meant to me-
> Life and Hope and Love and You
> (And you did not see them grow
> Where his mangled body lay,
> Hiding horror from the day;
> Sweetest, it was better so.)

> Violets from oversea,
> To your dear, far, forgetting land

These I send in memory,
Knowing You will understand.

In early May, the first of Roland's men was killed.
Describing to Vera how he had found him, 'lying very
still at the bottom of the trench with a tiny stream of
red trickling down his cheek onto his coat', Roland
proceeded to remonstrate with himself for bringing the
reality of war closer to her.

Vera's response to the war, and her reaction to all
Roland was telling her, showed a marked ambivalence. She
could express her horror at the lengthening casualty lists
from the battle of Neuve Chapelle, and her compassion
for the 'shattered bodies' of wounded men, while at the
same time be writing to Edward about how 'thrilling' she
found Roland's letters. '… I feel I should give anything to
be there with him!', she wrote to her brother. 'I quite envy
you … Somehow it seems as if to die out there wouldn't
be so very hard as it would anywhere else.'

Roland's telling postscript to a letter to Vera, dated
21 April, showed the extent to which his ideals of honour
and glory, and heroism in the abstract, were already
wearing thin after little more than ten days' experience of
trench life. 'There is nothing glorious in trench warfare',
he observed despondently. 'It is all a waiting and a
waiting and taking of petty advantages – and those who
can wait longest win. And it is all for nothing – for an
empty name, for an ideal perhaps – after all.'

Back in February, in her first overt criticism of the
war, Vera had questioned Roland about whether the
call of King and Country was really the call of God, as

soldiers and civilians were so often being told. Now she went further and asked him whether anything could justify 'all the blood that has been & is to be shed':

> The terrible things you mention & describe fill me, when the first horror is over, with a sort of infinite pity I have never felt before. I don't know whether it is you or sorrow that has aroused this softer feeling – perhaps both … Is it really all for nothing, – for an empty name – an ideal? Last time I saw you it was I who said that & you who denied it. Was I really right, & will the issue really not be worth one of the lives that have been sacrificed for it?

Roland made no direct answer to her question. For Vera, this perception all at once clouded over, and she admitted in her diary that 'I am not sure that I agree myself in all I said to him.'

In fact, Vera's continuing dependence on rhetoric of patriotism and martial heroism is evident in her response to the posthumous appearance of Rupert Brooke's famous sonnet cycle, *1914*. The five war sonnets had recently been published in book form (following Brooke's death from blood poisoning in the Aegean, while sailing to the Dardanelles with the Royal Naval Division), and immediately had a profound effect on Vera. They were 'all sad & moving, in spite of their spirit of courage & hope', she noted, after listening to the English tutor Helen Darbishire reading them out loud to a small group of students, one evening at Somerville, '& through them all ran a strangely prophetic note, a premonition of early death.' Furthermore, Brooke's image as a warrior-poet inevitably fused with thoughts of Roland, for whom she enclosed copies of four of the sonnets in her next letter.

Even Somerville had succumbed to the war effort. Vera returned to Oxford for the summer term of 1915 to find that the War Office had requisitioned the college buildings as a military hospital – where both Siegfried Sassoon and Robert Graves would later be patients – and that most of the students and dons had moved to Oriel College's St Mary Hall quad (Vera was among a small number of undergraduates who were allocated rooms at Micklem Hall, off the High Street).

Attempting calmly to work for her next batch of exams seemed almost an impossibility, with news of the war constantly overshadowing everything and her anxiety for Roland dominating her thoughts. Instead of doing her work, she told Roland, 'I sit dreaming over it, thinking of you among barbed-wire entanglements.' Her tutor, Hilda Lorimer, formerly so distant and critical, appeared more sympathetic now. Miss Lorimer's attitude to events outside Oxford was less insular than that of some of her colleagues. Her favourite brother had been killed in Persia in 1914, and she would later serve as a hospital orderly in Salonika.

Vera might no longer be interested in her college work, but she resolved none the less that she 'must do it without feeling interested. Such is the only form of courage I can practise.' However, throughout the spring of 1915 she had been considering another option: to abandon her studies and become actively involved in some form of war work. Government propaganda was beginning to put pressure on women to participate in the war effort, freeing men from their peacetime occupations and allowing them to enlist. Already, during the Easter vacation, Edith Brittain had faced criticism, from another Buxton matron, of Vera's failure to take up voluntary nursing, unlike some other young women of the town. At one point Vera considered registering at a Labour Exchange for clerical work, 'a sort of service' that appealed to her 'far more than merely to swell the number of superfluous housemaids [which is how she still looked upon voluntary nursing].' She even started to learn to type as preparation for office work.

Why then in the end did she decide to nurse? Most obviously, her immediate motivation derived from her love for Roland. It was her need to empathise with him and his sacrifice that made her choose the female war service demanding the hardest work and 'the most wearying kinds of bodily toil'; one that, if she ever succeeded in being posted to a frontline hospital, would bring her as close to the dangers of the conflict as it was possible for a woman to be.

But in applying to nurse, Vera was also responding to the widely accepted parity between the public school educated men who volunteered for Kitchener's Army and the socially privileged women who became Voluntary Aid Detachment nurses. For these middle and upper class women, longing for a wartime identity beyond the passive role of knitting for the troops or living vicariously through their male relatives, the figure of the volunteer nurse – as opposed to her professional counterpart – with the sign of the Red Cross emblazoned on her chest, and public perception of her heroism, appeared as a clear answer to their needs.

The Voluntary Aid Detachment programme had been founded in 1909 to provide voluntary aid to the sick and wounded in the event of an invasion. By 1915, the scheme had been greatly expanded to cope with the severe shortage of professional nurses caused by the unforeseen effects of trench warfare. VADs were provided as probationary nurses, paid and housed by the military authorities. Once accepted, following a month's probation, the VAD signed a six-month contract. In addition to an allowance for food, washing and travel, the volunteer nurse was paid £20 a year for the first seven months, with increments of £2.10s for each subsequent six-month period. The pay may have been less than what the average domestic servant received, but this did not stand in the way of a rush of recruitment in the early period of the war, when as many as 600 voluntary nurses a week were being appointed to military hospitals at home and abroad. Most VADs, in any case, did not need the money, and looked for no financial reward. They were expected to be of an equivalent social class to male commissioned officers, and, while there were plenty of VADs from lower down the class structure, most of them conformed to this middle or upper class pattern.

Vera's decision to leave Somerville in order to nurse, initially for a year, was accepted by Emily Penrose, the College Principal. On 17 June, Vera took Pass Mods (in July she would receive a letter from Miss Lorimer congratulating her on her well-deserved success). Ten

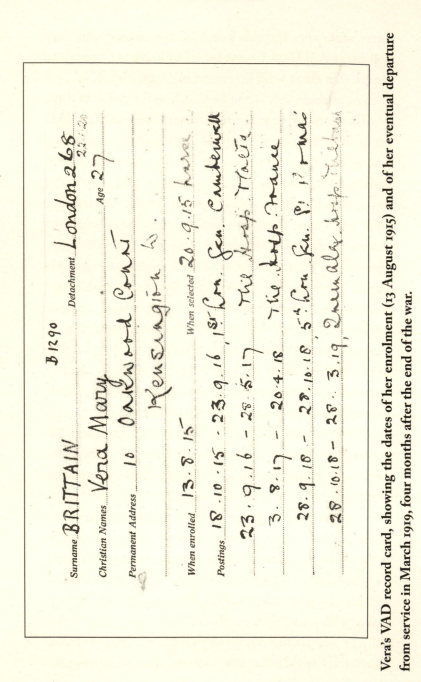

Surname BRITTAIN   B1290   **Detachment** London 268

Christian Names Vera Mary   **Age** 27

Permanent Address 10 Oakwood Court
Kensington W.

When enrolled 13.8.15   **When selected** 26.9.15 home

Postings 18.10.15 – 23.9.16, 1st Lon. Gen. Camberwell
23.9.16 – 28.5.17   Mil. Hosp. Malta
3.8.17 – 20.4.18   Mil. Hosp. France
28.9.18 – 28.10.18, 5th Lon. Gen. B. 1st mob.
28.10.18 – 28.3.19, 2nd Lon. Gen. Hosp. Chelsea

Vera's VAD record card, showing the dates of her enrolment (13 August 1915) and of her eventual departure from service in March 1919, four months after the end of the war.

days later, she started work as an unpaid auxiliary Voluntary Aid Detachment nurse at Buxton's Devonshire Hospital, a short walk down the hill from 'Melrose'.

She would work at the Devonshire for the next three months, attempting in the meantime to sign on as a VAD under contract at a military hospital. It was a gruelling nine-hour day. At the outset Vera's duties included making beds, cleaning and serving meals. Before long she was allowed to dress minor wounds while undertaking some other aspects of basic patient care. As so often, she demonstrated a seemingly inexhaustible desire to prove herself in whatever task she set herself, however menial. She had never worked so hard in her life. Vera's pre-war existence had been largely cloistered and protected from mundane drudgery – at the start of her nursing career she was unable even to boil an egg – but this new experience was providing her with 'a little insight into the lives of those who always have to work like this.' She imagined that caring for her British Tommies at the Devonshire was like nursing Roland by proxy, and nurtured the dream that he might be invalided home with some slight wound, allowing her 'to look after him & thoroughly spoil him.'

On 18 August, Vera finally received the news for which she had waited for so long: after nearly five months at the Front, Roland was coming home on a week's leave. Two days later they were reunited in the first class ladies' waiting room at London's St Pancras Station. Roland looked older and thinner. In his time away, Vera noted sadly, he had acquired 'a premature air of having knocked about the world'. At first, owing to his short-sight, he barely recognised her. Then they shook hands and stood looking at each other, somewhat awkwardly. She could scarcely believe that standing before her was the flesh and blood reality of the man who had appeared at times to exist for her solely through the written word and her imagination. Roland's sense of dislocation was even greater. Indeed, returning to England, after months in the trenches, must have seemed to him like coming to another planet, with precious little time to readjust before he went back again,

The barrier of reticence increased the tension between them, and this in turn was exacerbated over the next few days by a sequence of tiring railway journeys. On the train to Buxton that evening to stay with Vera's parents, Roland proposed marriage to her. Vera's response, despite her acknowledgement of her deep feelings for him, was to assert a sense of her 'best self', and with it, of her independence and autonomy. She declined an announcement of the engagement in *The Times*, or a formal request by Roland to her father for her hand in marriage. The next day they agreed after further discussion to consider themselves engaged, though with Vera's additional proviso that she would not wear a ring. However much the conventional side of her was attracted by the thought of wearing an engagement ring, she saw the custom as a survival of the days when a wife was regarded as her husband's possession. It was a symbol of the old inequality, '& therefore hateful to me'.

Returning to St Pancras the next day, en route to Lowestoft, they had lunch with Edward and Victor Richardson. It was the first occasion on which

Uppingham's Three Musketeers had been together since the outbreak of war, more than a year earlier, and, unlike Roland, neither Edward nor Victor had succeeded in getting to the Front. Edward had experienced serious disappointment, confidently expecting to be posted to France on several occasions since the spring, only to be kept back, having fallen foul of his commanding officer in the Sherwood Foresters, who had developed a strong dislike of him. In the meantime, Victor had almost died from an attack of cerebrospinal meningitis, the illness that had killed his mother, and would only be fit enough for light duties on home service at the Woolwich Arsenal towards the end of the year. Both men, therefore, listened intently to Roland's first-hand experience of life at the Front. Roland went into technical detail about the barbed wire entanglements in front of the trenches, and spoke about the shooting of sentries who fell asleep on duty.

At the Leightons' cliff-top house at Lowestoft – darkened according to the black-out regulations because of its position as a conspicuous landmark for Zeppelins or ships out at sea – Marie Leighton regaled Vera with stories of Roland's childhood, dabbing at her eyes with a handkerchief as she did so. The other members of the household, the younger children, Clare and Evelyn, and their father Robert, gathered round to examine Vera with open curiosity. Mrs Leighton seemed to have accepted the existence of another woman in her son's life. 'I am very fond of you', she told Vera during one of these long confessionals, 'but I *do* want any woman that gets him to care for him so very much – just as I have done.' Roland meanwhile hovered in the background, silent and detached.

His and Vera's one moment of intimacy that weekend occurred as they walked alone on a cliff path, the afternoon before their departure. Sitting down 'on a soft dry bed of heather', they looked out at the 'vast grey shadow' covering the sea, as Roland silently put his arm around her and drew her close to him. He gently played with the wisps of Vera's hair that were blowing over her face and after a time rested his head on her shoulder before kissing her. There was 'such a painful joy & a joyful pain', she remembered afterwards, knowing that they had been together in life so little and were soon to part again. 'There, on that dark heather-covered cliff beside the sea, I realised the depth & strength of my own passion – realised it & was afraid.'

As Vera had to report for duty back at the Devonshire on 24 August, and Roland was not returning to France until the end of the week, they had agreed that he should see her off at St Pancras. They spent their final hours together on a shopping expedition in London. Vera had herself measured for a VAD coat, in preparation for her orders to a military hospital; Roland bought himself a 'vicious-looking' steel dagger in case 'the fierce excitement & madness of hand-to-hand fighting' ever arose. She was depressed by the sight of the dagger in his hands, and, watching him write out the cheque to pay for it, found it incongruous that a person 'with such artistic hand writing should have use for a thing like that.'

But the warrior's mask slipped during their last minutes together. 'He said very bitterly that he didn't *want* to go back to the front, and this glimpse of England and real life had made him hate France more than ever.'

Vera tried to commit his features to memory, realising that in just a short time 'they would only be an image in my mind':

He stooped & kissed me passionately almost before I realised he had done it ... He looked away from me a moment & dragging out his handkerchief furtively drew it across his eyes. I hadn't realised until then that this quiet & self-contained person was suffering so much ...

The whistle sounded & the crowd moved a little away from the door. But he still stood close to me and as the train began to move he pressed my hand almost violently, and, drawing my face down to his, kissed me again, more passionately than ever. And I kissed him, which I had never done before, and just managed to make myself whisper "Goodbye." He said nothing at all, but turned quickly from me and began to walk rapidly down the platform ... He never turned again. What I could see of his face was set & pale.

The resumption of routine life, at the hospital and in the trenches, proved more difficult after their time together. She cherished the bitter-sweet memory of his arm round her and of his bristly head on her shoulder, and told him of her 'insane impatience' to be kissed by him again. A return to the written word as their means of communication, however, came as something of a relief for both of them. 'We both seem less reserved in letters,' Roland observed, 'more like our real selves'.

By early September, Roland and his battalion were in France, in trenches in the Hébuterne sector, between Amiens and Arras. From here he sent Vera a melancholy description of his surroundings. In earlier months, he had derived some comfort from the ways in which pastoral elements of the landscape co-existed with the destruction of war, however incongruous that sometimes appeared. But now the sight of an old trench, 'disused and overgrown with grass, with dug-outs fallen in or wrecked by shells, and here and there a forgotten grave and rusty bayonet', depressed him. In such conditions, he admitted, England and Vera seemed very far away.

The gulf between Roland's heroic conception of war and its reality was growing. Back at the beginning of August, before his leave, Roland had confessed to Vera that, whereas he had once talked of 'the Beauty of War', experience had taught him 'that it is only War in the abstract that is beautiful', and that 'Modern warfare is merely a trade'. Now, in a letter to Vera, written a fortnight after his return to France, he delivered his most sustained, powerful and damning condemnation of the war – and specifically of the kind of rhetoric, extolling the chivalric values, and elevated abstractions, of patriotism, honour and sacrifice, even holiness, that were to be found in the war sonnets of Rupert Brooke.

Nowhere is Brooke's name mentioned, but the echoes of 'The Dead', Brooke's third sonnet, quoted with bitter irony, make Roland's intention plain. While superintending the building of some dug-outs, Roland had chanced upon the remains of some dead Germans, 'the fleshless, blackened bones of simple men who poured out their red, sweet wine of youth ...':

> Let him who thinks that war is a glorious golden thing, who loves to roll forth stirring words of exhortation, invoking Honour and Praise and Valour and Love of country ... let him look upon a pile of sodden grey rags that cover half a skull and a shin bone and what might have been Its ribs, or at this skeleton lying on its side ... and let him realise how grand & glorious a thing it is to have distilled all Youth and Joy and Life into a fetid heap of hideous putrescence. Who is there who has known & seen who can say that Victory is worth the death of even one of these?

In her reply to Roland, Vera acknowledged that the war could only be justified 'if it puts an end to all the horror & barbarism & retrogression of War for ever.' But at the same time her diary reveals how limited was her understanding of what he was trying to tell her. Her dependence on precisely the kind of rhetoric Roland was attacking is clear in several passages where she quotes, completely without irony, from Brooke's sonnets. Later, she would write to Roland that Brooke's lines about pouring out the red, sweet wine of youth keep coming into her head as she contemplates the wounded in her ward. Roland had once sent Vera violets from 'Plug Street Wood', knowing that she would understand. However, the gap between her sentimentalised conception of the war and his first-hand experience of it was deepening, and potentially the cause of a new kind of barrier of incomprehension was coming between them.

It would at least have helped to alleviate his boredom if Roland had been involved in some actual fighting, rather than spending day after day sitting in a ditch, taking the occasional shot 'at a more or less docile and usually invisible enemy who is content to do the same.' In late September there seemed at last some chance of this and Roland warned Vera that his section of the line might be involved in a major British attack. But it was a false alarm, and the ill-fated and costly Battle of Loos took place without the 7th Worcesters playing any part in the fighting.

One consequence of the heavy influx of casualties from Loos was that after a long period of waiting Vera's orders to commence nursing at a military hospital finally came through. On 18 October she left Buxton and arrived at the nursing hostel on Champion Hill in south-east London, ready to begin work at the First London General in Camberwell the next day.

A converted teachers' training college, the First London General was the military wing of St Bartholomew's Hospital, and Vera's was the second attachment of VADs to arrive there. This was nursing-proper. Her patients were often the seriously wounded or dying, and Vera had rapidly to accustom herself to 'the butchers' shop appearance' of the wards and the 'holes in various parts of people that you could put your fist into'. The hours were longer – often 12½-hour days at a stretch – and the living quarters spartan and inadequately equipped, with just one bathroom for 20 occupants. The

Vera as a VAD at the First London General Hospital, Camberwell.

military-style discipline and regulations represented a marked contrast to anything Vera had experienced so far, their strictness reflected in the Red Cross specifications for the VAD uniform: collars were to be stiff, white, 2⅛ inches deep; cuffs stiff, white, 3⅜ inches deep; belts stiff, white, 3 inches deep. Anything that smacked of individualism was to be stamped out. Additionally, Vera was to experience something of the friction between VADs and the professional nurses, who regarded these novices with hostility and resentment, and were both wary of entrusting them with serious responsibilities and concerned that after the war they might be competing with them for jobs (with state registration still several years away, trained nurses suffered from understandable concern about their professional status).

Vera's initial probationary month at the First London General left her barely any time to keep up with her diary, though she continued to be conscientious in ensuring that Roland never went short of regular letters. His letters, by contrast, were becoming more intermittent. In the third week of October, just as she was starting at the new hospital, he wrote apologising for his cruelty in having kept her letterless for so long, while admitting that he was becoming immersed in his world at the Front as the only way of stifling 'boredom and regrets'.

Vera responded acerbically – she had already warned Roland that she could be much harsher with her pen than in person – asking him not to get '*too* absorbed in your little world out there – even if it makes things easier'. His silence throughout the next few weeks was broken only by a cool, impersonal note in which he commented on his 'metamorphosis' into 'a wild man of the woods, stiff, narrowed, practical'. His next letter was scarcely any better. He asked if he seemed like 'a phantom in the void' to her; she seemed to him 'rather like the character in a book or someone whom one has dreamt of & never seen'.

This was too much for Vera. 'Most estimable, practical, unexceptional Adjutant', she replied, before going on to admit that she was unable to write as freely as she wanted in case it should be the last letter he ever read. All the same she reminded him with brutal frankness that the war killed other things besides physical life, and that she sometimes felt 'that little by little the Individuality of You is being as surely buried as the bodies are of those who lie beneath the trenches of Flanders and France'.

This brought a reply from Roland full of penitence and remorse. He had been 'a conceited, selfish, self-satisfied beast'. They were reconciled, and his letters became once more warm and vital. Nevertheless, they continued to display an oddly dispassionate quality, as if he was looking in at their relationship from the outside. In one, he went some way towards admitting that he had fallen in love with Vera as the incarnation of an ideal, Lyndall, the feminist heroine of his favourite novel, *The Story of an African Farm*. 'Apropos of which I may remark that the unfortunate Olive Schreiner is too often made responsible for things over which she had no control whatever.'

Roland had managed to obtain Christmas leave from 24 to 31 December. 'Life seems quite irradiated now when I think of the sweet hours that may be ahead', Vera wrote to him on 7 December, barely able to contain her excitement at the news. Ten days later she wrote to Roland to confirm that the Matron of her ward had given her leave at the same time as his. 'And shall I really see you again – and so soon?' Her parents had recently taken up residence at the Grand Hotel in Brighton, following Arthur Brittain's decision to take early retirement from the paper mills. The Leightons were also nearby. They had let the Lowestoft house, and had rented a cottage at Keymer, seven miles outside Brighton. The plan was that Roland would spend Christmas Day with his family and be reunited with Vera on Boxing Day.

At the Grand Hotel Vera waited impatiently for news of Roland. Having received no message from him on Christmas Day, she assumed that his crossing had been delayed, or that communication by telephone or telegram had been difficult, and went to bed expecting to hear from him the next day.

The following morning Vera had just finished dressing when she was called to the telephone. She 'sprang up joyfully'. However, the voice on the other end of the line wasn't Roland's as expected, but his sister Clare's. And the purpose of her call was not to tell Vera that Roland had arrived home, but that he had died of wounds, after being shot through the stomach by German sniper fire while repairing the wire in front of a trench, at a casualty clearing station, on 23 December.

It would take months for Vera and Roland's family to piece together the circumstances of his death. Hardest for Vera to bear would be the absence of any final message from Roland in his last hours.

What did eventually reach her was the manuscript of Roland's poem 'Hédauville', probably his last, and undoubtedly his finest effort. Dated November 1915, from the period of their epistolary estrangement, and recalling their walks in countryside around Buxton, the spring before the war, the poem seemed strangely prophetic, but of exactly what?

The sunshine on the long white road
That ribboned down the hill,
The velvet clematis that clung
Around your window-sill,
Are waiting for you still.

Again the shadowed pool shall break
In dimples round your feet,
And when the thrush sings in your wood,
Unknowing you may meet
Another stranger, Sweet.

And if he is not quite so old
As the boy you used to know,
And less proud, too, and worthier,
You may not let him go –
(And daisies are truer than passion-flowers)
It will be better so.

Was Roland foreseeing his own death and predicting that Vera would meet someone else? Or was he trying

> December 25. 1915.
> Christmas Day
>
> (Deeply grieved to forward following Telegram)
> T.223 Regret to inform you that
> Lieut. R. A. Leighton 7th Worcesters died
> of wounds December 23rd Lord Kitchener
> expresses his sympathy Colonel of Territorial
> Force — ¾Records, Warwick (George.)

> "They shall not grow old, as we that are left
>   grow old,
> Age shall not weary them, nor the years
>   condemn,
> At the going down of the sun and in the
>   morning
> We will remember them."

The text of the telegram to Roland's family, informing
them of his death, copied by Vera into her notebook,
together with quotations from Laurence Binyon's poem of

"Fear no more the heat of the sun
Nor the terrible winter's rage..."

remembrance, 'For the Fallen' ('They shall not grow old...'),
and Shakespeare's *Cymbeline*.

gently to suggest that their love, so difficult to sustain in wartime, was cooling and that Vera will eventually find happiness elsewhere?*

There was of course no way she could ever know. Vera's own poetic response to Roland's death (and the favourite among modern readers of all her war poems) gives a stark picture of her grief and heartbreak, and remains affecting despite, or because of, its 'numbed banality':

(TO R.A.L. DIED OF WOUNDS IN FRANCE,
DECEMBER 23ʳᵈ, 1915)

Perhaps some day the sun will shine again,
And I shall see that still the skies are blue,
And feel once more I do not live in vain,
Although bereft of You ...

But, though kind Time may many joys renew,
There is one greatest joy I shall not know
Again, because my heart for loss of You
Was broken, long ago.

---

* Harry Ricketts (*Strange Meetings. The Poets of the Great War*) has recently lent some credence to this latter view by pointing out that Roland's poem is an imitation – in subject matter, stanza form, and its extra delaying line in the final verse – of Rupert Brooke's 'The Chilterns'. Brooke's poem had ended with 'a brisk brush-off' to some former girlfriend: 'And I shall find some girl perhaps/And a better one than you,/With eyes as wise, but kindlier,/And lips as soft, but true./And I daresay she will do.'

3 To the Bitter End   1916–1918

As she struggled to come to terms with the shock of Roland's death, Vera poured out her feelings into her diary and letters. The return to his family, in mid-January 1916, of Roland's belongings – including the uniform in which he had been killed – became the subject, in both a diary entry and a lengthy letter to Edward, of some of Vera's most moving and memorable writing. Her instincts as a writer, and the power of her observation, confronting the truth head on without restraint, reasserted themselves even as she battled to cope with her grief.

She had been paying a visit to the Leightons at Keymer, and arrived 'at a very opportune though very awful moment.' Roland's possessions from the Front had just been unpacked and were lying all over the floor. 'Everything', she told Edward, 'was damp & worn and simply caked with mud'.

And I was glad that neither you nor Victor nor anyone else who may some day go to the front was there to see. If you had been you would have been overwhelmed by the horror of war without its glory. For though he had only worn those things when living, the smell was the smell of graveyards & the Dead. The mud of France which covered them was not ordinary mud; it was not the usual clean smell of earth, but it was as though it was saturated with dead bodies – dead that had been dead a long, long time … There was his cap, bent in and shapeless out of recognition – the soft cap he wore rakishly on the back of his head – with the badge coated thickly with mud. He must have fallen on top of it, or perhaps one of the people who fetched him in trampled on it. The clothes he was wearing when wounded were those in which he came home last time. We discovered that the bullet was an expanding one. The hole where it went in front – well below where the belt would have been, just beside the right-hand bottom pocket of the tunic – was almost microscopic, but at the back, almost exactly where his back bone would have been, there was quite a large rent. The under things he was wearing at the time have evidently had to be destroyed, but they sent back a khaki waistcoat or vest … which was dark and stiff with blood, and a pair of khaki breeches also in the same state, which had been slit open at the top by someone in a great hurry – perhaps the Doctor in haste to get at the wound …

Unable to bear the sight – or smell – Marie Leighton ordered her husband to remove Roland's clothes, and burn or bury them. They detracted from his memory, she declared, and spoilt his glamour. Using kettles of boiling water to melt the frozen earth, Robert and Clare Leighton buried them in the back garden.

Vera's grief at Roland's death was intensified by the absence of a final message from him, apart from the enigmatic poem in an exercise book returned with his blood-stained belongings. Additionally, she was distressed that his death appeared not to have served any military purpose. Wasn't there a curious rashness, she asked herself repeatedly, about his decision to go out to mend the wire in front of a trench in such bright moonlight? And might this be defined as the act of heroism to which he had so long aspired, or was it merely folly? She received the news of Roland's recent conversion to Roman Catholicism, a decision he had kept from both her and his family, with fewer misgivings. She was glad after all that he had had some hope of a life in the next world during his last months in this one.

Whatever the doubts that continued to possess her, Roland's death had left Vera with an overwhelming need to go on believing that he had died for some larger purpose, and that the war was being fought for some definite end. 'I do condemn War in theory most strongly', she wrote in early 1916, '... but there are worse things even than War and I do believe even wholesale murder to be preferable to atrophy and effeteness. It is better to do active harm and definite wrong than to drift and make no effort in any direction ... And when the War in question is a War *on* War, all the usual objections are changed into the opposite commendations.'

The timing of Edward's departure for France with the 11th Sherwood Foresters could hardly have been worse. Six weeks after Roland's death, following many

"Goodnight, sweet friend, goodnight,
Though life and all take flight
Never good-bye."

An early photograph of Roland's grave at Louvencourt (marked by the large cross in the foreground), before the construction of the cemetery there, pasted by Vera into her notebook. The lines of verse are from W. E. Henley's 'Echoes XLII', a favourite poem of Roland's. A quotation from them was to be inscribed on his headstone.

delays and false alarms, Edward was seen off at Charing Cross by his mother and Vera. Once in the trenches, he described his early impressions of his new life for his sister's benefit. He now understood, he wrote, how Roland had been killed: 'it was quite ordinary but just unlucky.' By the end of March, Edward and his battalion had moved to the town of Albert, on the Somme, with its famous Golden Virgin and Child leaning from the spire of its basilica (one of the most powerful myths among British troops was that the war would end when the statue fell). From here, one evening at the beginning of April, Edward cycled to Louvencourt to visit Roland's grave. Removing his cap in front of the grave, he prayed that he might be worthy of Roland's friendship. But he didn't remain there long, unable to feel that 'He' was present (like Vera, Edward had begun to apotheosise Roland in their correspondence).

In Edward's absence, the third member of the Uppingham Triumvirate, Victor Richardson, assumed a new significance in Vera's life. Still stationed at Woolwich Arsenal on light duties following his recovery from illness, Victor met Vera regularly for dinner in London at the Trocadero, where he provided a sympathetic ear for her problems. It was Victor who attempted to unravel the sometimes contradictory accounts of Roland's death that Vera was receiving, and to reassure her that his life had not been thrown recklessly away, telling her that it was the duty of a good officer to safeguard his men by going ahead to inspect the wire in front of a trench, to see that all was safe before the rest of the wiring party followed. Victor more than lived up to his nickname of 'Father

Confessor' as he counselled Vera with compassion and understanding.

Another friend of Edward's, Geoffrey Thurlow, a fellow officer from his original battalion, also offered her friendship and solace. Educated at Chigwell School, in Essex, Geoffrey was up at Oxford for one term, in the autumn of 1914, studying at University College, before he decided to enlist. As a second lieutenant in the 10th Sherwood Foresters he had befriended Edward, and their friendship survived their separation when Geoffrey was sent out to France ahead of Edward in October 1915.

Vera had met Geoffrey Thurlow when he spent a weekend in Buxton, shortly before she left home for the First London General, and had immediately been struck by him. She described him as 'strange, though very pleasant looking', with close-set blue eyes, a decided chin, and thick, wavy brown hair. Geoffrey had sent her a brief but heartfelt letter of condolence from France on learning of Roland's death. Not long afterwards, Vera learned from *The Times*'s casualty list that Geoffrey had been wounded in action southeast of Ypres. In late February 1916, she visited him while he was recovering in bed at Fishmongers' Hall Hospital, near London Bridge.

Geoffrey's face wound was healing, but he was clearly suffering from the after-effects of shock. Vera found him 'very interesting to talk to', as she reported to Edward, though both of them were constrained by shyness and reserve. Several days later, Vera returned for another visit, on this occasion with her mother. This time Geoffrey was sitting up in a chair, huddling over a small gas stove to ward off the chill. He talked openly of the German attack in which most of his men had been killed, and of being virtually surrounded; and agonised over his decision whether to retreat or face certain death. Later, when he knew Vera a little better, he was to confess to her that he felt forced to overcome his 'funk' in order to fight, and that he believed himself to be of no 'earthly use' as an officer, being 'disgustingly windy' and lacking in courage.

Geoffrey's candour about such matters must have made a deep impression on Vera. Most officers felt an obligation to present themselves to the outside world as completely fearless. As the psychiatrist of war neurosis, W. H. R. Rivers, was to note in 1918, according to the 'social standards' of the day, 'fear and its expression are regarded as reprehensible'. Vera was also aware that Geoffrey was 'a non-militarist at heart', as she described him in her diary, who had put aside his objections to war 'for Patriotism's sake'. As their friendship grew, so did her respect for him. On her third visit to the hospital, Geoffrey overcame his reticence and asked Vera to accompany him to a concert at the Queen's Hall during his convalescent leave. After he was passed fit and returned to France in August they would write frequently to one another with an increasing sense of intimacy and understanding.

Vera's friendships with Victor Richardson and Geoffrey Thurlow were vital in relieving her sense of desolation in the period immediately following Roland's death, as she began to make uncertain plans for her future. She had returned to Camberwell on 3 January, far too soon after Roland's death, and immediately found hospital work intolerable and almost impossible to bear. She was depressed and often lonely, irritated by the petty restrictions imposed on VADs, and seriously considering giving up nursing when her contract expired in April. The uninspiring tasks she had once undertaken with such dedication as an expression of solidarity with Roland were now carried out cursorily or not at all. Off-duty she lay for hours thinking about Roland, going over in her mind 'all the times I saw Him & all the details of His death until there seems nothing worth having left in the future at all; it is a shame that everything worth while should come to an end so soon in one's life.'

She continued to vacillate about whether to continue nursing, and went so far as to make arrangements to rent a room in Bayswater in anticipation of taking a clerical position at the War Office. A visit to Somerville in early March also confirmed in her own mind that she could not return to Oxford until the war was over.

Finally, though, she decided to remain at Camberwell. She was not quite 'the erratic weathercock' she seemed, she explained to Edward, for no sooner had she made her mind up to leave 'than the growing conviction came over me quite against my reason, that somewhere He was living still, and knew and disapproved'. In order not to remain at Camberwell indefinitely, Vera, together with Stella Sharp, her old school friend from St Monica's days, who was also serving as a VAD at the First London General, put her name forward as a volunteer for foreign service. In a matter of weeks, or more probably months, she could expect to be sent to any one of several destinations: Egypt, Salonika, Malta or, as she fervently hoped, France.

In the meantime, there would be more than enough work to occupy her at Camberwell. At the beginning of June, Edward returned to England on leave. During his forty-eight hours in London, after lightning visits to his parents in their new, rented accommodation at Macclesfield, to Victor at Purfleet, and to the Leightons at Keymer, he revealed to Vera that his leave was preparatory to a new 'show'. 'He spoke in veiled but significant language of a great battle – another Big Push – soon to take place, and knew that he was to be in it. He said that it would be somewhere in the region of Albert, where he is now'. At the end of June, the First London General received orders to release all convalescents and prepare for a great influx of wounded. At Camberwell, they knew that a tremendous bombardment had begun from the heavy vibration of the guns beneath their feet, echoing across the Channel. On 1 July, as they emerged from Southwark Cathedral following a performance of Brahms's *Requiem*, Vera and Stella Sharp were met by the sight of newspaper placards proclaiming 'GREAT BRITISH OFFENSIVE BEGINS'. It was the first day of the Battle of the Somme.

Sick with apprehension, Vera busied herself with the arrival of the first convoy of wounded. Victor was with her at the weekend, giving her what reassurance he could. On 4 July, Vera found a pencilled note from Edward in the hospital letter rack informing her that he had been wounded in the left arm and right thigh, 'not seriously', and that he hoped to come to England. The next day, as

Vera wrote in a hurried entry in her diary, 'There was an early morning convoy of officers into J [ward] ... I saw Miss George, who ran up to me & said "Do you know your brother's in J?" *Edward* in J! ... It was like some impossible novel that he should have come to *my* hospital'.

For the next three weeks, before Edward left Camberwell for a protracted period of convalescence, Vera was at his bedside as often as her nursing duties would permit, piecing together the story of his experiences on the Somme.

Early on the morning of 1 July, Edward had led his company in the first wave of the attack that was to go down in history as one of the most terrible days of slaughter in the history of the British Army: suffering 57,470 casualties, of whom almost 20,000 were fatalities in a single day. While his company was waiting to go over the top, the wounded from an earlier phase of attack began to crowd into the trenches. Then part of the regiment in front began to retreat, throwing Edward's men into panic. Edward had to return to the trenches twice to exhort them to follow him over the parapet. About 90 yards along No Man's Land, Edward was hit by a bullet through his thigh. He fell down and crawled into a shell hole. Soon afterwards a shell burst close to him and a splinter from it went through his left arm. The pain was so great that for the first time he lost his nerve and cried out. After about an hour-and-a-half, he noticed that the machine-gun fire was slackening, and started a horrifying crawl back through the dead and wounded to the safety of the British trenches.

For 'conspicuous gallantry and leadership during an attack on Mouquet Farm near Thiepval', on 1 July, Edward was awarded the Military Cross. 'Isn't it unspeakably splendid about Edward's Military Cross!', Vera wrote to her mother in August, on receiving the news. In a sense, it seemed a reversal of expectation that Edward, sensitive and peace loving, should have distinguished himself in battle, when Roland, who had been so desperate for military glory, had gone to his death in circumstances devoid of heroic limelight. Victor believed that there was no warring side to Edward's nature and that he was sustained by duty alone. Certainly the strain on Edward quickly began to show, and after the first day of the Somme he appeared to have aged ten years.

It is especially telling that Vera's contemporary response to Edward's experiences on the Somme shows no trace of anger or bitterness. Indeed, at one point she writes of 1 July as 'one of the greatest dates in history'. Her focus is exclusively on her brother's heroism, and she finds no place to question the uses to which his heroism had been put. This attitude is confirmed in the poem 'To My Brother', which Vera wrote two years later for the anniversary of 1 July. With its profusion of militaristic imagery, its martial excitement, and its hero-worship, 'To My Brother' is essentially a pro-war poem:

Your battle-wounds are scars upon my heart,
Received when in that grand and tragic 'show'
    You played your part
    Two years ago,

And silver in the summer morning sun
I see the symbol of your courage glow –
> That Cross you won
> Two years ago.

Though now again you watch the shrapnel fly,
And hear the guns that daily louder grow,
> As in July
> Two years ago.

May you endure to lead the Last Advance
And with your men pursue the flying foe
> As once in France
> Two years ago.

Roland's death had confirmed him in Vera's eyes as the embodiment of the ideal of 'heroism in the abstract'. Now Edward's bravery on the Somme provided her with another personal example of heroism and self-sacrifice. As Vera contemplated foreign service, she wrote that she would strive to live by such values – and if necessary to die by them as well.

Her overseas posting was to Malta. On 24 September 1916, Vera set sail on the *SS Britannic*, the converted sister ship of the *Titanic*, as part of a convoy of nursing sisters and VADs. Accompanying her was Stella Sharp, who had also been ordered to Malta. It was Vera's first extended experience of foreign travel, but, despite the magnificent sights, including a visit to Naples with its museum full of discoveries from Pompeii, and a view of the Greek island of Skyros where Rupert Brooke is buried, passengers and crew lived in constant fear of being torpedoed by a German submarine (just two months later, the *Britannic* would be sunk by a torpedo with the loss of 50 lives). At Mudros, the port where they trans-shipped to the *Galeka*, a small liner that would take them into the Grand Harbour at Valletta, Vera leaned over the ship's rail and thought about Roland, wondering whether she would ever return to England, 'or if I should not, & so complete the tragic story.' She would not mind if that turned out to be the case, and perhaps it might be an appropriate conclusion – 'only I want to write so much.'

In fact, rather than being blown out of the water, Vera was one of 16 VADs who succumbed to a serious epidemic of food poisoning. She was carried off the ship on a stretcher and spent her first three weeks in Malta at Imtarfa Hospital, seven miles from Valletta, in the centre of the island. It was not until the last week of October that she was judged fit enough to be discharged to begin work at St George's Hospital, two miles from Valletta, situated just above St George's Bay. Here she and the other nurses occupied a two-storied converted army barracks built of stone. In her diary, where the entries were becoming more sporadic, Vera described St George's as 'a most beautiful hospital, built on a peninsula running right out into the sea.' The sea was right below the rocks, with 'a delightful little bay' that was so close that Vera and other VADs could go down to swim from their rooms, wearing mackintoshes to cover their bathing suits.

Malta had become an important hospital base for the British army in the course of the Gallipoli campaign,

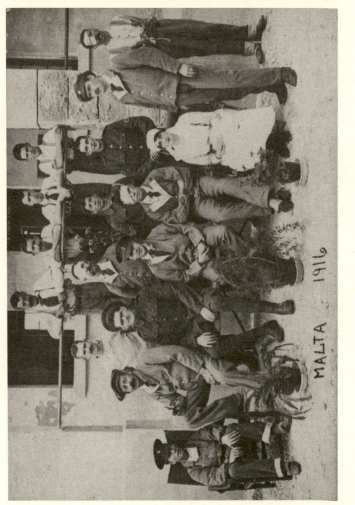

Vera with a group of her patients at St George's Hospital, Malta.

and by 1916 there were some 29 hospitals and convalescent homes on the island. At St George's, sick patients,
suffering from dysentery, enteric fever and malaria, as
well as from diseases of the eye, ear, nose and throat,
easily outnumbered the wounded. Yet while there was
the same number of patients as at Camberwell (though
with a smaller nursing staff to care for them), the
working conditions were much better. There was greater
informality, with a relaxed dress code. No one seemed
very particular about uniform, and VADs were permitted
to wear soft low collars and panama hats. 'The difference
between the stiffness & starchiness of the Nursing
Profession in England and the free & easiness here', Vera
wrote home to her mother, 'is quite remarkable.' Nor was
there much evidence of hostility between professional
nurses and VADs. 'The Sisters treat you as friends &
equals instead of as incompetent underlings.' In contrast
to the strict rules in the London military hospitals,
VADs at St George's were in charge when the Sister
was off duty, they wrote reports, took temperatures and
pulses and distributed medicines. In one letter to Edith
Brittain, Vera wrote proudly that she was in sole charge
of the block (a block had an upper and lower floor with
three wards on each), with only an orderly on hand to
assist:

At the 1st London we always had to be on with a
Sister … but they trust you much more here – in fact
they have to, because there are not enough Sisters to
go round … Do you remember how afraid I used to
be of thunder when I was little? Now I feel quite a

'Lady of the Lamp' marching along with the thunder crashing … to see if other people are afraid!

Off duty, the social life offered by governmental and naval society was full of diversions. There were picnics and garden parties, including one at the Governor's palace, and invitations to tea and tennis. Vera enjoyed many of these, although she sometimes wondered whether they were 'appropriate to the present state of affairs'. She found it difficult to be among people who remained untouched by 'all the unhappy things in this war', an attitude that played its part in separating Vera from her old school friend Stella Sharp, who had no such misgivings about enjoying herself and was fortunate enough not to suffer any personal bereavement for the duration of the war.

Most of all, though, the beauty and mystery of Malta itself were breaking the hold of the intense spell of grief that had enveloped Vera since Roland's death. In the brilliant light, the glorious sunrises and sunsets, and the beautiful and unfamiliar flower life of the island, Vera was discovering a strangely reinvigorating affirmation of life. Nevertheless, at Christmas 1916, as she prepared to mark the first anniversary of Roland's death, she observed that making yourself used to living without a person was like managing with your left hand if you lost your right, but that she missed 'Him as much as I ever did & always shall'.

Anxiety for those at home experiencing Zeppelin raids, or in France on the Western Front, was never far away, and Vera's apprehension was increased by regular delays to the mail, leading her to make both Edward and

Mrs Brittain promise to send cablegrams in the event of bad news. Edward remained out of harm's way, engaged in home duties at Brocton Camp in Staffordshire, but Geoffrey had returned to France in early August, seen off by Vera and Edward from Liverpool Street. In October, not long after Vera's arrival in Malta, a letter from Edward contained the surprising news that Victor had succeeded in getting to the Front by transferring from a Territorial battalion to the 9th King's Royal Rifles.

Roland's death had imbued both Victor and Geoffrey with a romantic aura in Vera's eyes. Victor, in particular, was compared by her to Sir Galahad, as a chivalric knight whose lord had fallen in battle. The disparity between the somewhat ethereal image of Victor that she had created, and the reality of a modern soldier adapting to trench life, was highlighted by Vera's reaction to Victor's letters from the Front, which began to reach Malta in November. Writing to Vera, Victor was cheerfully optimistic about his new life in the trenches, describing life in the dugouts as very comfortable, and regretting that he was unable to send her reports of anything more 'gruesome' or 'thrilling' than his discovery of 'a very few very dead Frenchmen in No Man's Land'. 'Really', he continued, 'I am beginning to agree with the Rifleman who when some dear old lady said "What a terrible War it is", replied, "Yes Mum, but better than no War'.

Evidently – though her letters to Victor have not survived – Vera did not measure the force of her reply. From Victor's response to what she wrote, in particular his sad little remark that '[i]t is quite awful to feel the silent contempt of those whom one regards as one's dearest friends', it's clear that she found his unqualified militarism at the very least distasteful. Much more palatable were Geoffrey Thurlow's declarations of his unsuitability as an officer. 'You say that you are not callous enough for a nurse', Geoffrey had written to her a month before she sailed for Malta. 'Personally I'm far too timid for this life and whenever a shell comes near me I'm absolutely petrified within and without.' In Geoffrey's letters, throughout the winter and early spring of 1916–17, Vera was discovering, beneath the shy exterior, someone of warm understanding with a sensitive mind, who was open about his lack of a martial temperament.

In early February 1917, Vera was moved to St George's only surgical block. None of the patients was seriously ill, and she filled her spare time by catching up on her reading, including the books that Edward had sent her from England. One of these was the recently published Report of the Commission on the disastrous Dardanelles expedition. As ever, Vera inclined to the more heroic view of events, helped by her reading of John Masefield's *Gallipoli*, with its emphasis on the 'grandeur' of the campaign and its portrayal of the valour of its fighting men, whom Masefield compared to Greek heroes. She could not help thinking that it must have been 'a very fine and wonderful thing' to have 'fought so gallantly for such a forlorn hope'; and she wished that Roland, if he had had to die, could have been killed defending Gallipoli's beaches.

Victor's letter to Vera of 24 March struck a rare note of cynical resignation, intimating that his battalion was on the verge of an attack and signing off with the fatalistic words, '[w]ell, Vera, I may not write again – one never can tell – and so, as Edward wrote to me, "it is time to take a long long adieu".' Three weeks later, in a letter to Edward, Vera wrote of her own sense of foreboding, as news was gradually filtering through of a great battle. 'The longer the war goes on', she admitted to him, 'the more one's concern in the whole immense business seems to centre itself upon the few beings still left that one cares about, & the less upon the general issue of the struggle.' The following evening, while she was on night duty, Vera received a cable from Edward, informing her that Victor had been dangerously wounded.

She cabled home immediately asking for more news, and four days later another cable from Edward reached her:

Eyesight probably gone may live

On 9 April, Victor had led his men in an attack on a heavily defended German entrenchment, known as 'The Harp', at Vimy Ridge, three miles north of Arras. Victor was hit in the right arm, had the wound dressed, and carried on. There was serious machine gun fire and soon afterwards Victor fell unconscious from a bullet to the head. Scarcely conscious, he lay for ten days critically ill in a Rouen hospital, before risking the sea journey to London for specialist treatment. His left eye was shattered and had to be removed. At first his right eye appeared undamaged, but closer inspection would reveal that the optic nerve had been severed.

When Victor had been with Vera the previous July, speculating about Edward's fate in the Battle of the

Somme, he had told her of his belief that he would never go to the Front, and she had responded by saying that she was glad to know that there would be someone left after the War, and that she would not be left alone. With this memory in mind, Vera began to formulate a plan to return to England. 'The burden of debt' that those who could not fight owed to men such as Victor made her feel that she would 'give up all the things I ever meant to do & to be if I could but repay him a little for what he has sacrificed'. Something else was motivating her too: the idea that in Victor's 'clear & reverent memory' of Roland, Roland seemed to live still.

She had got no further with her plans when, on 1 May, two further cables containing devastating news reached her in quick succession. The first informed her that Victor's sight was hopelessly gone. The second – delivered an hour later – told her that Geoffrey had been killed in action on 23 April, at Monchy-Le-Preux, three miles south-east of Arras, in an attack on the Scarpe. During fierce fighting, Geoffrey had left the comparative safety of his trench and had gone out on top where he was almost immediately hit in the left lung by a German sniper. Under heavy bombardment, he was brought back into the trench and placed on a stretcher. Gazing intently at the orderly, Geoffrey uttered not a word and died about fifteen minutes later. Captain Daniel, Geoffrey's company commander, believed that he would not have suffered much pain, and would have experienced a feeling of slight suffocation.

Geoffrey's body was placed in a shallow area of trench, and the spot was marked until the padre could give him a proper burial. However, after the fighting was over the body had disappeared and was never found.

Three days before his death, Geoffrey had written a letter to Vera which she received on the evening of the day that the cable arrived with the news of the death. It was the kind of farewell letter, Vera told Edward, that she wished she had had from Roland. Geoffrey had written of the beauty he saw around him, even in the shell-torn landscapes of the Western Front. He observed the way in which the setting sun was reflected in the water at the bottom of the many crump holes, 'making them look [like] masses of gold.' And he ended this final letter to Vera with a renewed expression of his fear, as he waited to go into battle, that he would fail 'at the critical moment as truly I am a horrible coward'.

Sitting on the rocks' edge in the front of the night quarters on 1 May, Vera suddenly resolved to go home 'for Edward's sake & Victor's, & if he wishes it, to devote my life to the service of Victor, the only one (apart from Edward, who is different) left of the three men I loved. For I loved Geoffrey …'. Aware of the strength of Geoffrey's religious faith, she could not feel that Geoffrey had gone so completely as she felt Roland had, and as she sat on the rocks she sensed she was not alone, but that Geoffrey was standing there all the time beside her.

Vera knew that she could comfort Edward in the loss of his friends as no one else could. 'I can feel his need of me as strongly across all these miles as if he had actually expressed it', she wrote to her Uncle Bill, her mother's younger brother. She had intended to continue nursing until the war was over – and had only just renewed her contract – but her priority now seemed clear. Her intention was to offer to marry Victor.

By 12 May, Vera's resignation had been accepted and she had permission to return to England. Ten days later she left Malta. 'I hated to go, for I had been very happy there.' The threat from submarine warfare had made sea travel too dangerous, and she returned by a complicated overland route that took in Rome and Paris. By 28 May she was back home, at her parents' new London flat at Oakwood Court, off Kensington High Street, relieved that she had arrived in time to see Edward, who, after almost a year's convalescence and home duty, would shortly be going out to France again.

Edward meanwhile had been keeping Vera informed about Victor's progress, which was promising. 'He is perfectly sensible in every way', Edward had assured Vera, 'and I don't think there is the very least doubt that he will live.' Victor had been told that he would probably never see again, but 'was marvellously cheerful'. He had been through some 'rather bitter' days, but had quickly rallied, and was attempting to learn Braille, and receiving visits from Captain Ian Fraser from St Dunstan's, the charity for blind servicemen. Captain Fraser had encouraged Victor to think of leading an independent life in the future, despite his loss of sight. Victor talked of entering the Church, or of becoming a schoolmaster.

For ten days Vera was in constant attendance at Victor's bedside at the Second London General in Chelsea, which specialised in treating servicemen with badly damaged eyes. Although they talked at first of nothing more consequential than the hospital routine and the visits of his friends, Victor's mental faculties did not appear to be in any way impaired. The matter of their future does not appear to have been touched upon, though her very presence there may have signified to Victor something of her intention. Certainly Victor's father Frank, and his aunt Miss Dennant (his mother's sister, whom Frank Richardson afterwards married), were aware of Vera's willingness to offer Victor 'a very close & life-long devotion if he would accept it'.

However, on 8 June, Victor's situation took a dramatic turn for the worse. In the middle of the night, he experienced what he described to the nurse as a click in his head, like a miniature explosion. He subsequently became very distressed and disoriented, and by the time his family and Vera reached the hospital he was delirious and unable to recognise them. On the morning of 9 June, a telephone call to Oakwood Court, where the Richardsons were staying with the Brittain family, informed them of Victor's death.

Later Vera wrote of her recognition of the limits of her magnanimity, and of the likelihood that Victor's death had spared them both from a relationship that would have become increasingly difficult to sustain. At the time, however, his death left her with a feeling of despair 'at not being allowed to do if not the best ... at any rate the hardest thing I ever thought of doing ... Not even to be permitted to 'do good' – that seemed too bitter an humiliation'.

Nine days after Victor's death, it was confirmed that he had been awarded the Military Cross 'for conspicuous gallantry and devotion to duty'. His funeral in the small cemetery at Hove, his home town, was accompanied by full military honours. The *Brighton Gazette* reported that:

> The gallant young officer was the eldest son of Mr. F. V. Richardson of 65 Wilbury Avenue, and 15 Cambridge Road, Hove. The cortege was met at the entrance of the cemetery by a bugle and drum band, under Drummer-Sergeant Pratt, and a firing party. The hearse passed on, and the squads followed a slow march. The coffin was enveloped in the Union Jack, and resting upon it were officer's cap and sword. The coffin bore the inscription: 'Lieut. Victor Richardson, King's Royal Rifles, died 9th June, 1917, aged 22 years'.

The common loss of their three beloved friends in just 18 months reaffirmed the bond between brother and sister that had survived unbroken since childhood. At first Edward had seemed distant and withdrawn on weekend leave at Oakwood Court at the beginning of June. But his letter to Vera, written a couple of days after Victor's death, expressed his love for her, even as he acknowledged that everything that had seemed of value in life had tumbled down like a house of cards. 'We started alone, dear child', he wrote in conclusion,

> and here we are alone again; you find me changed, I expect, more than I find you; that is perhaps the way of Life. But we share a memory which is worth all the rest of the world, and the sun of that memory never

sets. And you know that I love you, that I would do anything in the world in my power if you should ask it, and that I am your servant as well as your brother.

Edward returned to France in the last week of June. Unable to face another railway station parting, out of superstition that this might ensure that they would never meet again, Vera said her farewells at Oakwood Court, and watched Edward's departure in a taxi from the windows of the flat before returning his violin to its case and putting the instrument away. Within weeks, Vera had returned to the VAD headquarters at Devonshire House to request a posting on the Western Front to be near Edward, and to fulfil her own 'small, weary part in this War' to the bitter end. She had broken her contract in order to return from Malta. But a sympathetic Red Cross official, learning that Vera had returned home to marry a man blinded at Arras, overlooked this breach of the rules, and arranged for her to join a small draft of nurses travelling from Dover to Boulogne at the beginning of August. On 4 August, the third anniversary of the outbreak of war, Vera arrived at Etaples, a small fishing port in the Pas de Calais, surrounded by windswept dunes and pinewoods, which had been transformed into the British Army's largest-ever hospital and reinforcement camp.

The 'Etaples Administrative District' provided not only hospitals but also prisons, stores, railway yards and port facilities, as well as infantry depots through which more than a million officers and men had passed, by September 1917, for regrouping and training on their way to the Front. The poet, Wilfred Owen, who was at Etaples at the beginning of 1917, and again in the autumn of 1918, just a couple of months before his death, remembered the place as a 'vast, dreadful encampment', 'a kind of paddock where the beasts are kept ... before the shambles'.

The first hospital at Etaples was opened in the spring of 1915. Two-and-a-half years later there were nearly 20 military hospitals, housed in timber buildings and under canvas. The vast encampment has been described as resembling a large town, or small city, several thousand of whose population changed on a daily basis.* Etaples was also the scene, during the second week of September 1917, not long after Vera's arrival there, of the British army's only serious mutiny of the war, when hundreds of young men demonstrated on the streets against the conditions in the camp, culminating in violent scenes on the Three Arch Bridge. One soldier, Lance Corporal Jesse Short, was quickly court-martialled and shot on a charge of incitement.

Etaples was to be the climax of Vera's nursing experience, representing real active service conditions at last. 'Well, Malta was an interesting experience of the world', she wrote to her mother on arrival, 'but *this* is war. There is a great coming & going all day long – men marching from one place "somewhere" in France to another, ambulances, transports etc passing all the time

---

* During August 1917, Vera's first month at Etaples, almost three thousand officers, and more than thirty thousand other ranks arrived there, while 2,432 officers and 51,707 other ranks were despatched to the Front from various depots.

… Everything of war that one can imagine is here, except actual fighting, & one can even hear the distant rumble of that at times'. The northern end of the camp contained a series of eight hospitals, and it was to one of these, No. 24 General, on the brow of a hill, extending in long lines of wooden huts at right angles from the road and interspersed with tents and marquees, that Vera found herself posted. She worked in a hut and slept under canvas.

The 24 General had been sent to France in 1915, and, by August 1917, formed the largest of the military hospitals at Etaples, with a capacity for accommodating 3,130 patients in its beds. Vera was quickly assigned to Ward 29, the centre for the treatment of sick and wounded German officers and men, which contained just over 400 patients at the time of her arrival. 'It was with very mixed feelings that I followed my guide to the German ward', she remembered in the draft of an article written the following year. 'To the majority of British people … the word "German" has gradually come to indicate not so much an individual as the personification of those powers of evil against which an heroic Army is striving to prevail'. To be 'cast into the midst' of a number of people, of 'hostile nationality', was therefore 'a slightly alarming experience'.

Yet she soon realised that it was impossible to feel any antipathy towards her German patients as they were far too ill, '& utterly dependent' on her, for that. In the operating theatre attached to the ward, the medical officer, assisted by a nurse, performed acute operations, while Vera and two orderlies dressed wounds – gunshot wounds penetrating the chest or abdomen, badly smashed heads and amputated limbs. More than half the cases were empyemas (a condition in which pus and fluid from infected tissue collects inside a body cavity).

The tragic and fundamental absurdity of the situation in which she might be involved in saving the life of a man, whom, a short time before, Edward could have been trying to kill, was not lost on her. From trenches outside Ypres, Edward observed that 'It is very strange that you should be nursing Hun prisoners, and it does show how absurd the whole thing is'. Vera saw the experience, as she wrote in an article for her old school magazine, as an opportunity to live up to the Red Cross motto, 'Inter Arma Caritas', reinforcing her conviction that a dying man has no nationality.

In the second week of September, Vera was transferred to a British hut specialising in acute medical cases. Here she watched in the early days of December as the first victims of mustard gas from the Battle of Cambrai began to arrive on the convoys. In a letter to her mother, dated 5 December 1917, which she afterwards described as her 'first angry protest against war-time hypocrisy', she drew attention to the plight of the pathetic, dying Tommies:

I wish those people who write so glibly about this being a holy war ... could see a case – to say nothing of 10 cases – of mustard gas in its early stages – could see the poor things burnt and blistered all over with great mustard-coloured suppurating blisters, with blinded eyes ... all sticky & stuck together, & always fighting for breath ... saying that their throats are closing &

they know they will choke. The only thing one can say is that such severe cases don't last long … and yet people persist in saying that God made the War, when there are such inventions of the devil about …

Like her nursing of German prisoners, Vera's care for mustard gas victims was contributing to her scepticism about the war, to the extent that she would later pinpoint this as the period when she began to think along pacifist lines and, more precisely – in the case of her mustard gas patients – as the moment when she 'definitely ceased to regard the War as an instrument of God or even of human justice.' But she was still a long way from taking a formal position against the war. Indeed, as a nurse serving close to the front line, it's difficult to see how she could possibly have done so, or how she might have developed these flashes of outrage into a sustained argument against the war. Moreover, the first shock and horror of the gas cases soon wore off. By February 1918, Vera was writing in a much more matter-of-fact fashion to her mother about 'the gassed cases' that were crowding into her ward. 'I find the work quite interesting & it is conveniently regular – I mean the treatment is practically the same for everybody so you can simply go straight through it.'

In an early letter home from Etaples, Vera had commented on the 'charmingness' of the other VADs and nursing sisters, while reassuring her parents that the women she worked with were all 'ladies', and of similarly middle or upper middle class origins. With one of the Queen Alexandra nursing sisters, Faith Moulson (later disguised as 'Hope Milroy' in *Testament of Youth*), who took charge of the German ward soon after Vera's arrival there, Vera was to establish a lasting friendship. With her calculated delight in shocking people by her outrageous remarks, her dramatic manner and mode of speech, and her 'half-scornful control of everything and everybody', Faith Moulson radiated unconventionality. Eight years older than Vera, Faith came from a long line of bishops – one uncle was the Bishop of Manchester – and had trained as a nurse as a rebuke to the clerical atmosphere of her family. She 'is quite my best friend here', Vera told her mother, 'quite a different type from the usual trained nurse as not only is she very clever & original … but she comes from a very good family …'. Off duty, they were constant companions, taking long walks, or drives in a fiacre throughout the countryside around Etaples, where the landscape 'is really lovely, especially on a stormy day, when the lights and the shades on the sand hills with their little clumps of dark pines, & the long expanse of sand & the distant sea are most beautiful.'

In the third week of January 1918, after just under six months' continuous ward duty in France, Vera was granted permission to return home, where Edward was also on leave. That autumn had been a harrowing time for him. In the mud and cold of the Ypres Salient, he had spent only three-and-a-half days out of the line, and experienced several close brushes with death. In November, Edward and the 11th Sherwood Foresters were suddenly posted to Italy, to join the Allied reinforcements on the relatively quiescent Italian front in the Alps above Vicenza. Following the humiliating rout of the Italian army at Caporetto, in October 1917, the task of breaking the Austrian offensive had assumed a new and pressing importance.

It was an unsatisfactory leave. After more than three years of war, Arthur and Edith Brittain were showing signs of breaking under the strain. Mrs Brittain seemed obsessed with the price of butter and the difficulty of obtaining good servants. Mr Brittain, with nothing else to do, brooded depressively about his health, having retired far too early for a man of his relative youth or vitality (he was barely 50 when he left the paper business). To add to this, Vera was confined to bed for a week with a feverish illness. By the time she had recovered, only three days' leave remained, during which she and Edward snatched a few visits to theatres and concert halls.

On 21 March, two months after her return to Etaples, the hospitals were overwhelmed with a new influx of wounded and dying men, as Ludendorff, the German commander, began a last desperate bid for victory against the Allied armies in the West. For three weeks, exhausted doctors, nurses and VADs worked frantically to cope with the never-ending rush of convoys, all the time suppressing the fear that the Germans might actually be in the process of winning the war.

However, by the second half of April it was clear that the German offensive would fail. But Vera would not be in France to witness the Allies' recovery. At the end of March, while the fighting was still at its height, she received a letter from her father informing her that, as her mother was in a nursing home with 'a complete general breakdown', it was her duty to leave France and return to Kensington immediately.

Family obligations were one area in which voluntary nurses and volunteer soldiers were clearly differentiated. A soldier on active service could not, of course, return home, however badly he might be needed by a family member. A VAD, by contrast, who did not face punishment for breaking her contract, or for deciding – as many did – that one six months term away from home was long enough, often bowed to family expectations to put their needs above those of the country. It wasn't uncommon for VADs to feel torn by a conflicting sense of duty, as the unmarried daughter felt forced to conform to the standards set by an earlier generation of women.

Vera gave in to parental pressure, though not without a terse reminder to her mother that, while she could put in an application to resign, it might be months before she was released. In the event, she arrived at Oakwood Court at the end of April, to find the flat empty and her father in a local hotel. She immediately brought her mother back from the Mayfair nursing home where she was staying and took charge of the household. But it was with a heavy air of resentment that she tried to readjust to the dull monotony of civilian life.

At the beginning of the third week of June, the newspaper headlines were dominated by reports of an Austrian offensive on the Italian front, during which there had been heavy fighting. Edward had not written since 3 June, and, as the days passed and no word came from him, Vera wandered restlessly around the flat, barely able to conceal her fear. Edith Brittain was staying with her mother at Purley, and Vera and her father were just finishing tea on the afternoon of 22 June when they were interrupted by a sudden loud knock at the door.

For a moment I thought that my legs would not carry me, but they behaved quite normally as I got up and went to the door. I knew what was in the telegram – I had known for a week – but because the persistent hopefulness of the human heart refuses to allow intuitive certainty to persuade the reason of that which it knows, I opened and read it in a tearing anguish of suspense.

'Regret to inform you Captain E. H. Brittain M.C. killed in action Italy June 15th.'

'No answer,' I told the boy mechanically, and handed the telegram to my father, who had followed me into the hall. As we went back into the dining-room I saw, as though I had never seen them before, the bowl of blue delphiniums on the table; their intense colour, vivid, ethereal, seemed too radiant for earthly flowers.

Reconstructing the events of that day for this account from *Testament of Youth*, written more than a decade later, Vera had no diary to rely on: it had petered out on her return from Malta a year earlier. Nor were there any letters to revive her memory: all her regular correspondents, apart from her mother, were dead. All that survived to remind her of that fateful afternoon were some faded stems from the blue delphiniums, dried and pressed within the pages of a notebook.

At three o'clock on the morning of 15 June, the Austrians had launched a surprise attack with a heavy bombardment of the British front line along the bottom of the San Sisto Ridge. Five hours later, the enemy had penetrated the left flank of Edward's company and had begun to consolidate its positions. Edward led his men in a counter-offensive and regained the lost positions, but while keeping a lookout on the enemy, a short time later, he had reportedly been shot through the head by a sniper and had died instantaneously. He was buried in his blanket with four other officers in the small cemetery at Granezza, 4,000 feet up in the mountains.*

Robert Leighton, Roland's father, endeavouring to offer some comfort to Edward's grief-stricken father – 'having passed through the same harrowing ordeal' – wrote of 'the proud consolation' that Edward had 'met his death gloriously in the hour of victory'. But Arthur Brittain would never recover from the loss of his son. Seventeen years later, he would take his own life by drowning in the Thames near Twickenham.

Numbed with grief – 'Not many women have suffered more than she has suffered in this war', as Robert Leighton noted – Vera reapplied to VAD headquarters for a further foreign posting. However, a change in the rules meant that a VAD who had broken her contract could not be sent abroad again without a further term

---

* For the mysterious circumstances of Edward's death, see the Afterword below, 'Ipplepen 269: The Tragic Fate of Edward Brittain'.

of 'grounding' at a home hospital. As a consequence, Vera would spend the remaining months of the war in London, first at St Thomas' Hospital, and then at Queen Alexandra's Hospital on Millbank. She would be 'demobbed' at the end of March 1919, four months after the Armistice.

Looking back on those last months of the war, she remembered that:

> Now there were no more disasters to dread and no friends left to wait for; with the ending of apprehension had come a deep, nullifying blankness, a sense of walking in a thick mist which hid all sights and muffled all sounds. I had no further experience to gain from the war; nothing remained except to endure it.

And yet the rebuilding of her life following the war was a remarkably rapid process, attributable to Vera's qualities of dogged endurance and self-belief, as well as to her ambition to be a writer, which, more than anything else, she later claimed, held her to life. In the spring of 1919, at the age of 25, Vera returned to Somerville after a four-year absence. Here she changed subject from English Literature to History, a reflection of her belief that a study of the recent past might help her to understand the events of the last four years.

But by now Vera was close to a breakdown brought on by a form of survivor's guilt, in which she suffered from the delusion that her face was disfigured. She was bitter, too, at what she regarded as the insensitivity of her younger Somerville contemporaries towards her war experiences. She was rescued and sustained by the friendship of another undergraduate, Winifred Holtby. Temperamentally and physically the two women were poles apart. Vera was small, dark and intense, and far from easy to know; Winifred was tall, blonde and gregarious. What they had in common was a desire to succeed as writers.

From Winifred's recognition of Vera's emotional fragility emerged a relationship that was to be mutually satisfying and beneficial. Winifred's warmth and generosity, her need to be needed, which was such a strong component of her personality, would sustain Vera as she rebuilt her life and attempted to fulfil her literary ambitions. Vera, for her part, would help to mould Winifred's future as a writer, as well as encouraging her commitment to working for peace and women's rights. In the autumn of 1921, after taking their Oxford finals, and travelling to Italy and France to visit the graves of Edward and Roland, they set up home together in Bloomsbury. They contributed pieces of journalism to a variety of publications, including the feminist weekly *Time and Tide*, and wrote fiction, and lectured for the newly founded League of Nations Union, which promoted the League's work for disarmament and international arbitration, and for the Six Point Group, in support of equal rights feminism.* It was the beginning

---

* It should be clarified here that, throughout the twenties and most of the thirties, Vera accepted that the controlled use of armed force, through internationalist solutions, might be necessary to prevent war. She did not

of a working partnership that would extend over the next 14 years.

In 1923, Vera published her first novel, *The Dark Tide*, earning herself a mild notoriety in the literary world – as well as a stinging rebuke from her former college – for its mocking portrayal of Oxford, Somerville and its dons. Another, less successful, novel, *Not Without Honour*, followed a year later. In June 1925, Vera married George Catlin, a political scientist. Loosely speaking, he was a member of the 'war generation', though illness had prevented him from reaching France until just before the Armistice, too late to fight. In more ways than one, he was 'Another Stranger', resembling the enigmatic figure in Roland's poem: his courtship of Vera was conducted largely by letter from America, and there were only limited opportunities for them to meet before their marriage. Moreover, Catlin, like Roland, was a Roman Catholic.

What George Catlin offered Vera was a marriage of equals, defined in feminist terms, and a generous acceptance of Winifred Holtby, Vera's 'second self', as she once referred to her, as the third member of their London household, an arrangement that worked especially well as Catlin was in the United States for half the year, teaching at Cornell University.

By 1930 they had two children: John Edward, born at the end of 1927, and Shirley Vivian, in the summer of 1930. Living in Chelsea, Vera had a life of relative

---

become a pacifist, with the absolutist conviction that it is wrong to take part in any war, until 1937 when she joined the Peace Pledge Union.

"I, too, take leave of all I ever had."

Lieutenant Roland Aubrey Leighton. 7th Worcesters.
(Died of wounds near Hébuterne, Dec. 23rd 1915.)
Buried at Louvencourt.
Lieutenant Victor Richardson M.C. 9th K.R.R.C.
(Blinded at Vimy Ridge, April 9th 1917. Died
of wounds 2nd London Gen. Hosp. June 9th 1917.)
Buried at Hove.
Lieutenant Geoffrey Robert Youngman Thurlow.
(Killed in action at Monchy-le-Preux, 10th Sherwood Foresters
April 23rd 1917.) Buried?

Captain Edward Harold Brittain. M.C.
(Killed in action leading his company 11th Sherwood Foresters in the
counter-attack in the Austrian offensive on
the Italian front, June 15th 1918.)
Buried at Granezza, Lusiana.

An 'In Memoriam' page to Roland, Victor, Geoffrey and
Edward from Vera's notebook. The line at the top is from
Robert Nichols's 'Farewell', one of the poems in his wartime
collection, *Ardours and Endurances* (1917).

domestic contentment, and intellectual stimulus, and companionship of a kind she had always aspired to, and one that would have appeared unattainable from the perspective of her Buxton years.

However, something of overwhelming significance continued to elude her: the successful completion and publication of a book about her war experiences. Only this, Vera believed, would exorcise the suffering of the war years, commemorate the young men she had lost, and ultimately bring her peace of mind.

4 'Didn't Women Have Their War As Well?' 1918–1933

After an hour of strenuous work she was in the annexe outside the ward for a moment, getting some fresh water to wash a patient, when hasty footsteps echoed down the passage, and a voice called agitatedly … She went outside the annexe immediately, to see a flushed and somewhat dishevelled Angell, who leant against the wall, and panted out, 'I say! Do you know your brother's in K ward!'

Pale as death with the sudden shock of reaction, Ruth stood for a moment quite unable to speak. At last she gasped out:

'Gabriel – in K! Angell, are you sure?'

'Sure! I should think I was! Why, I've just been bathing him. You can imagine what I felt like when I came to take off his tunic, and saw the name on his label.'

'Is he badly wounded?' asked Ruth excitedly …

'No, not very badly', was the reply. 'It's his foot, I think a fractured ankle … Oh, and there's a nasty little wound on his right hand, but that's not serious.'

[…]

A waving arm in a blue pyjama sleeve summoned her, from a bed beneath one of the tall windows; in another moment she was by his side. Around them the work of the ward continued hurriedly and somewhat noisily, but to Ruth everything seemed wrapped in a great stillness in which she and Gabriel were alone. She only wanted to see him, touch him, know that he was safe. He was pale, but very cheerful in the joy of release from strain. She noticed with a shock that in the four weeks since she had seen him, he seemed to have aged five years. His uninjured left hand lay clasped in hers, and she sat listening while he talked excitedly, finding relief in words from the burden of recollection.

'I couldn't get the men to go at first. Some Hun had shouted "Retire!" and part of the regiment in front of us came back in a panic. I made them follow me in the end, all the same. This knock on the hand didn't worry me, but I couldn't get on after my foot was hit. I yelled to them to carry on, though … I never knew what dead men could look like before I was in the midst of a whole heap of them. One was turning all green and yellow … I dreamed about that for a night or two' …

> As he talked on Ruth became aware of subtle altera-
> tions in Gabriel … He had come too close to the
> horror of the great conflict to regard it any longer as
> an ideal war, but he had by no means lost his powers
> of idealization.

This passage, describing the reunion of a VAD nurse
with her brother, who has recently been wounded during
the fighting on the first day of the Battle of the Somme,
is instantly reminiscent of a similar meeting recounted
in *Testament of Youth*, and, further back still, of Vera
Brittain's diary account of coming upon the wounded
Edward at her hospital, the First London General, in
July 1916.* Yet, as is evident from the brother's and sister's
Christian names, it belongs to neither. Instead the scene
is taken from one of the many fictional treatments of her
war experiences which Vera wrote in the period from the
end of the war to the late 1920s.

In the foreword to *Testament of Youth*, published in
1933, Vera described her original idea for her war book
as that of a long novel. She never got much further than
planning it as it turned out to be 'a hopeless failure': 'I
found that the people and the events about which I was
writing were still too near and too real to be made the
subjects of an imaginative, detached reconstruction.'

In fact this is a massive oversimplification of the
creative process that led eventually to *Testament of Youth*.
For a bewildering number of plans and drafts of different
novels centring on the war and Vera's experiences exist;

---

* For a brief excerpt from the diary account, see above, p. 78.

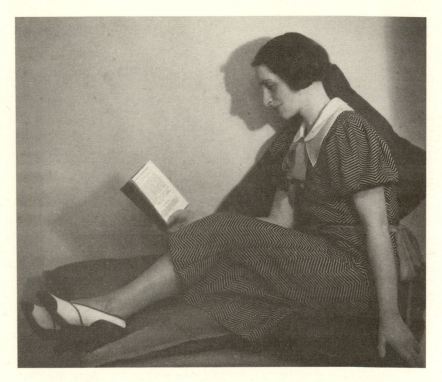

A publicity photograph of Vera in 1933 taken for *Testament of Youth*.

most of the drafts are difficult to date with any precision; some break off *in medias res*, while others appear to have reached completion even where a complete draft apparently no longer exists.

As far back as March 1916, Vera had written to Edward that '... if the War spares me, it will be my one aim to immortalise in a book the story of us four ...' (at that time her friendship with Geoffrey Thurlow, the fifth member of her wartime circle, still lay in the future). We know from Vera's diary that, in the months following Roland's death in December 1915, she wrote a short story about their relationship, though this appears to be no longer extant. However, her first attempt at a sustained work of fiction was based on life at the 24 General. Returning from Etaples in April 1918, and confined to her parents' flat, Vera decided to embark on a novel about her hospital experiences in France while her impressions of her time there were still fresh. The novel's original title was 'The Pawn of Fate' – in 1924 it was revised and retitled 'Folly's Vineyard' – and its plot revolves around the relationship between a young VAD, Sybil Beresford (or Veronica, as she is called in some parts of the book), an obvious attempt by Vera at a self-portrait, and an eccentric senior nursing sister, Hope Milroy, based on Faith Moulson, the sister in charge of the German ward at 24 General in 1917.

The first part of the novel, set at 'Echy', includes moving descriptions of nursing German prisoners in terms that are almost identical to the pieces of journalism on the same subject that Vera was writing in the closing months of the war: 'The more Sybil pitied them, the more acutely she felt the tragedy of war. It seemed to her that she and they alike were victims, broken by the desire for domination of that military caste which had plunged Europe into disaster.' In its concluding chapters, though, the plot takes a sudden sensational lurch towards melodrama, as Hope Milroy is raped by Basil Raynor, a hospital surgeon, gives birth to a child back in England, and commits suicide, leaving her daughter to be brought up by Sybil Beresford.

The knowledge that the Hope Milroy story was to some degree taken from real life, and that Basil Raynor also had a prototype at Etaples, led Roland's parents, Robert and Marie Leighton, to advise Vera to delay publishing the novel. Robert Leighton, with his experience as a publishers' reader, admired the hospital sections but did not see how Vera could eliminate 'the very human story of Sister Milroy' without damaging the structure of the book as a whole. Mrs Leighton thought the novel 'too good as it is to lose', and advised Vera 'to write it as you thought it & hold it back.' Vera was not discouraged, as she already had another novel in mind: 'the hero will be taken from you', she wrote to Edward on 4 June 1918, 11 days before his death, '& I don't suppose you'd have me up for libel!'.

In the meantime, Vera had been preparing her war poetry for publication by Erskine Macdonald, an 'experimental publisher' of distinctly dodgy credentials, using a subsidy from her father in the form of ten reams of 'antique printing paper'. *Verses of a V.A.D.*, which appeared in late August 1918 with a foreword by Marie Leighton, contains Vera's first published observations about the First World

War. Predominantly elegiac and documentary in subject matter and tone, the collection included 'Perhaps', written in Roland's memory, and 'To My Brother', completed four days before Edward's death, as well as poems in memory of Victor and Geoffrey. Many of the *Verses* had been written during rushed breaks from the hospital routine. In September 1917, for example, Vera reported that she had been writing a poem about the German ward 'while watching a patient who was rather sick come round from an operation'. Among the other published hospital poems were tributes to two nursing sisters at Etaples, whom Vera mildly hero-worshipped, not only Faith Moulson but also Sister 'Mary' from the medical ward at Etaples where Vera nursed in 1917–18. Two poems, 'The Sisters Buried at Lemnos' and 'Vengeance is Mine', commemorating the nurses killed in the German air raid on Etaples in May 1918, a month after Vera's departure from the camp, anticipate one of the major themes of *Testament of Youth*, the concern that feats of female heroism in the war should not go unrecorded.

Yet, despite the fact that Vera's awareness of the human cost of war is very much to the fore in some of these poems – in 'May Morning', for instance, she refers to the 'ruin' and 'individual hell' that 'only War can bring' – there is none of the bitterness, anger or indignation against the war that was so strongly to characterise her later reflections. 'The German Ward' may contain glimmerings of Vera's future pacifism, or at least of her latent internationalism, when she writes of what she has learned from nursing enemy prisoners ('that human mercy turns alike to friend or foe/When the darkest hour of all is creeping nigh'). But these are effectively snuffed out by the appearance, further on in the sequence, of 'To My Brother', with its bold martial spirit and appetite for military glory. Where bitterness is certainly manifest is in two poems written by Vera following her return to Oxford in 1919 (and not therefore published in *Verses of a V.A.D.*). 'The Lament of the Demobilised', and 'The Superfluous Woman', express her post-war desolation and the beginnings of a sense of her own personal betrayal by the war.

The flat at 52 Doughty Street, in Bloomsbury, which Vera shared with Winifred Holtby after coming down from Oxford in 1921, was a hive of literary activity. Here they wrote – and rewrote – their first novels, Vera's *The Dark Tide* and Winifred's *Anderby Wold*, read what the other had written and provided constructive criticism and mutual support.

In 1922, in their first year at Doughty Street, Vera submitted typed selections from the diary, or 'Reflective Record', which she had kept between 1913 and 1917, for a publisher's competition offering a prize for a personal diary or autobiography. Entitling her selections 'A Chronicle of Youth', she reduced the length of the diary by almost a half, replacing all the names by pseudonyms, and cutting the text short at April 1916, soon after Roland's death and a year prior to the diary's actual conclusion. In doing so Vera was able to shape the narrative as a tragic love story, ending it climactically with the death of Roland (or Vincent Farringdon as he is called here) and her consuming grief for him. In a foreword Vera wrote that she hoped that the diary would remind readers of the extent of 'that despair which wasted so much youthful vitality and darkened the sunshine of the sweet years'. She continued, '[c]ould we but have a few more records like these to aid the imagination of the militarist and the sceptic, I believe that there would be few left who would be willing to condemn another generation to endure what this one has endured'.

The diary was not chosen, though reading it again in the course of making her selections helped to provide Vera with the plotline of her second novel, *Not Without Honour*, based on the pre-war struggles at Buxton of the rationalistic curate, the Reverend Ward. At the end of 1923, Vera made enquiries of her publisher Grant Richards about the possibility of publishing a war novel, presumably 'Folly's Vineyard', the revised version of 'The Pawn of Fate'. Richards was as encouraging as he could be given the publishing world's uncertain attitude towards books about the war, but it was not until February 1926, following Vera's marriage and temporary move to the United States to be with her husband, that she made further concrete proposals for a war novel in a letter to Winifred. This novel was to be called 'The Incidental Adam', and she intended to write it 'very quickly, without having to look up anything except my letters and diaries'.

Vera envisaged the book's main theme as that of youth betrayed into cynical disillusionment, set against 'a particular background of time and place.' But by May of that year she had progressed little further and was still 'aching, at long last, to write about the war, all the grieving and the struggle and the loss'.

'The Incidental Adam' was more broadly conceived as a narrative of a woman's development over a decade, showing the heroine through her relationships with various men, 'who are only incidental to what she believes to be her chief purpose in life'. Its concluding chapter was to have demonstrated that love, through a happy marriage entered into in accordance with principles of feminist equality, was not incompatible with a woman's work; and, moreover, that a woman could be 'set free', not by the 'repression' of 'the sex element', but by the 'reasonable satisfaction' of it.

However, in the discarded drafts of other novels from this time, the war theme is much more central. 'The Stranger Son' focuses on the 'Problem of Pacifism' and dramatises the clash between 'the desire to serve one's country and the belief that war is wrong', through the story of Vincent Harlow. Vincent declares his pacifist principles on the outbreak of war in 1914, and his father threatens to disinherit him as a consequence. This doesn't deter Vincent from expressing his disgust at the 'blood thirstiness and perversion of truth' that he witnesses at a recruitment meeting, or his acute disappointment, as someone with strong religious beliefs, at the attempted justification of the war by the established church. At the climax of the book, a local mob search out Vincent and violently humiliate him. The novel's conclusion finds Vincent working as a conscientious objector on a farm in northern England.

'The Stranger Son' is the only projected war novel that survives in which Vera seems to be deliberately writing away from her own experience. By contrast, 'The

Kingdom of Endurance' – or 'Youth's Calvary', or 'The Great Explanation', to give the novel its alternative titles – is much closer to fictionalised autobiography. Indeed, at the outset it bears a very close resemblance to the early sections of *Testament of Youth*. Virginia Dennison (Vera's fictional alter ego, also the name of the heroine of *The Dark Tide*) is the daughter of Robert, a 'hard-headed' businessman, the director of the 'famous Dennison china-firm', and Mildred, his wife, who originates from the 'poverty-stricken family of an obscure professional singer'. As a child, Virginia possesses a remarkable flair for storytelling, regaling her younger brother Anthony with bedtime stories, while the young Anthony demonstrates pronounced musical gifts ('music alone had power to arouse the enthusiasms slumbering beneath the surface of his calm disposition'). The setting of the story, Vera stated in her preface, with questionable veracity, 'is fictitious'; 'a considerable number of its characters', she had to admit, though, were 'deeply rooted in truth.'

'The Kingdom of Endurance' describes itself as a story of 'early passionate hopes & ardent aspirations … crucified to the grey crosses of a stricken age.' The epigraph on the title page – 'Redemption is from within, and neither from God nor man; it is wrought out by the soul itself, with suffering and through time' – is taken from the book so beloved of Vera and Roland, Olive Schreiner's *The Story of an African Farm*; and, in keeping with this, the novel embodies themes of self-sacrifice and suffering. But it also offers a message of the possibility of resurrection and rebirth in the wake of personal disaster. The author assures us in her preface that for those like

Virginia Dennison who have 'suffered and lost' there is 'a word of hope: RESURGAM'.

Structurally and narratively, 'The Two Islands', an incomplete novel about the wartime relationship between a brother and sister, Gabriel and Ruth Barrington, is the most coherent of all Vera's fictional versions of her war experiences. The book contrasts 'the sombreness of the Grey Island' (Britain) with 'the brightness of the Gold' (Malta), but portrays the deepening shadow that war casts over both of them. When war breaks out, Ruth is studying at the Slade School of Fine Art (where Roland Leighton's sister Clare was a student in 1922–23). She realises that 'the only way to endure war at all [is] to take part in it', and leaves the Slade in order to nurse as a VAD.

Ruth is in love with Lawrence Sinclair, a brilliant young journalist, who volunteers immediately and goes to the Front, where his illusions about the war are quickly shattered. 'I fancy this War before it's over will leave a good many people's dreams in the dust', he tells Ruth when he comes home on leave as 'quite a veteran warrior'. When Ruth's brother Gabriel also prepares to leave for France, Lawrence warns her that '[h]e won't find the glamour of a medieval crusade out there.'

Lawrence is killed at Loos, and Gabriel becomes 'the only hope of her future.' Despite his role as a thinly disguised Roland Leighton, Lawrence is little more than a cipher in the novel, perhaps because Vera was still wary of how Roland's family, and especially his dominating mother, would react to Roland's appearance in a book by her. Marie Leighton had become even more possessive of her son in death than she had been while he was alive, and, barely a month after Roland was killed, had persuaded the *Sphere* magazine to publish Roland's love poem to Vera, 'Violets from Plug Street Wood', while encouraging the entirely false impression that its romantic sentiments were meant for her. Six months later, in June 1916, Mrs Leighton published anonymously *Boy of My Heart*, a short memoir of Roland, and an emotional – and at times embarrassingly mawkish – valediction to the son she had worshipped. The book, its publishers testified, was 'a record exact and faithful, both in large things and small, of the short years of a boy who willingly and even joyously gave up his life and all its brilliant promise for the sake of his country'. The reviewer in the *Times Literary Supplement* squirmed with the 'uncomfortable feeling' that he was 'unduly prying into experiences much too intimate for publication'.

More significantly, the focus of 'The Two Islands' on the close bond between Ruth and her brother Gabriel – rather than on the Roland character – is undoubtedly a reflection of the fact that, of all Vera's wartime losses, Edward's was by far the most painful and the one which time could do least to heal. One of Roland's character-istics, as a poet, has been transposed to Gabriel, but in other respects Gabriel is a portrait of Edward Brittain. He possesses Edward's calm, imperturbable nature, his immaculate appearance, even under pressure (Edward had been nicknamed 'Immaculate of the Trenches' by fellow officers, and, on leave in London, Gabriel worries that his boots are 'rather bright' after he has wiped the

Somme mud from them), as well as Edward's professed difficulties with women.

Ruth volunteers for foreign service and is posted to Malta. Gabriel meanwhile is awarded the Military Cross for his bravery on the Somme, and following a period of convalescence is sent to Salonika, where he is seriously wounded by a gunshot through his head at close quarters. Gabriel arrives at Ruth's hospital in Malta, but dies after an unsuccessful operation. Ruth accepts a place in a large draft of nurses leaving for the Western Front. Before she goes, she visits Gabriel's grave at Pietà Military Cemetery, just outside Valletta (which Vera herself had visited in 1917, in order to pay her respects at the grave of a Buxton neighbour, Jerry Garnett, who had died at Gallipoli). The final scene of the novel, planned but never written, was to have depicted Ruth leaning over the ship's rail as it sailed out of Valletta Harbour, watching 'the tawny island' disappear below the horizon.

In common with Vera's other fictional versions of her war experiences, 'The Two Islands' is impossible to date reliably. However, yet another set of ideas for a novel, beginning just before the war and concluding in the decade following, began to materialise towards the end of the twenties, and, with this, one enters a more definite time frame. According to Vera's account in *Testament of Experience*, the sequel to *Testament of Youth*, the birth of her first child, her son John, in December 1927, encouraged her to think again about committing her memories to paper, at the very least for his private edification when he was grown up.

It must have taken extraordinary perseverance, after so many frustrated attempts, to return to writing about the war; but in the course of 1928, or early 1929, Vera established the structure and major themes of her new book. Nominally the book is still fiction, although the autobiographical intent could not be clearer:

Chapter 1 Provincial English town before the War – tennis – badminton club.

Chapter 2 Oxford – Provincial Hospital – London in war-time. Early love, generous, spontaneous, passionate, uncalculating. Background the early part of the War – with high hopes & idealism.

Chapter 3 London – Malta – London. The 'carry-on' spirit of the war. Hope gone; spirit of dogged determination left. Sacrifice still possible.

Chapter 4 The lowest ebb of the War – France – summer of despair – London in war-time again. Sense of youth over. Nov. 11th. The Armistice came too late to save anything from the wreckage.

Chapter 5 Oxford. The problem of the lost demobilised … have feeling of retarded lives, of lost time that will never be caught up, of being overtaken by the young, cocksure, undamaged people. Have experienced too soon & learnt too late.

Two matters intervened to delay Vera's progress. The first, at the beginning of December 1929, soon after she started writing the opening chapter, was the discovery that she was pregnant again. The second was a change in the literary climate. The successful publication of works by

This ultimately became "Testament of Youth"

This Was Their War. (or ~~when The Vision~~ Died).

~~The Incidental Adam~~ (novel.)

Prelude. Elaine. 1912.

Phase I.

Chapter 1. Jeremiah. 1933.

Chapter 2. ~~Empire~~ Rupert. 1914 - 1915.

Chapter 3. Edward and ~~Garry~~. 1916 - 1917.

Intermezzo.

Chapter 4. John ~~Point~~ Richard. 1917 - 1918.

Phase II.

Chapter 5. Gregory. 1919 - 1920.

Chapter 6. ~~Philip~~ Francis. 1922 - 1923 - 1924.

Chapter 7. Basil Vincent. 1924 - 5.

~~Conclusion~~ Finale. Elaine. 1927.

Vera's plan for 'This Was Their War' (originally 'The Incidental Adam'), one of the fictional versions of her war experiences. The novel would have included Roland's poem 'Hédauville' ('The sunshine on the long white road …').

(Right) Vera Brittain circa 1898
(Below left) Edith and Arthur Brittain
(centre and right)
(Below right) Edward and
Vera Brittain

(Above left) Revd Joseph Ward, curate of St Peter's, Fairfield
(Above right) Roland Leighton, circa 1913
(Below) 'The Three Musketeers': (L to R) Edward, Roland and Victor

(Above left) Edward Brittain
(Above right) Roland Leighton drilling his platoon, Peterborough, 1915
(Below left) Victor Richardson
(Below right) Geoffrey Thurlow

(Above) Vera as a VAD, Buxton, 1915
(Below) Vera, St George's Bay, Malta, 1916

(Above) *Gloria*, the ballet inspired by *Testament of Youth*
(Below left) Cheryl Campbell and Peter Woodward as Vera Brittain and Roland
Leighton in the BBC-TV adaptation of *Testament of Youth*, 1979
Below right) Shirley Williams outside her mother's home, 'Melrose', Buxton, 2008

(Above) Vera (Alicia Vikander) with Edward (Taron Egerton) before the war in scene from the BBC Films/Heyday Films production of *Testament of Youth* (Below) The 'Three Musketeers' at the Uppingham Speech Day. (From left, secon row) Roland (Kit Harington), (first row, second from left) Victor (Colin Morgan and Edward

(Above left) Vera at Oxford reading the casualty lists
(Above right) Geoffrey (Jonathan Bailey)
(Below left) Vera with the blinded Victor
(Below right) Vera as a VAD

(Above) Roland picks a violet in Plug Street Wood
(Below) Roland and Vera during Roland's final leave

such writers as Blunden, Sassoon and Graves, beginning in 1928, suddenly guaranteed war books a popularity even more emphatic than the indifference previously shown them, and would influence Vera's decision to write her war book, not as fiction but as autobiography.

The boom in war books that began a decade after the Armistice has sometimes been compared to the breaking of an emotional dam, or the outpouring of a flood. It began, though, as a trickle: 1928 was the year of publication of Edmund Blunden's autobiography, *Undertones of War*, and Siegfried Sassoon's skilfully fictionalised *Memoirs of a Fox-Hunting Man*, the final section of which deals with its hero George Sherston's early war service in France. The end of 1928 also saw the first performances of R. C. Sherriff's claustrophobic trench drama *Journey's End*, which became a sensation when it transferred to London's West End early the following year. However, 1929 was the point at which the dam finally burst and the spate of war books in Britain reached their numerical peak: 29 were published that year, including the appearance in March of the English translation of Erich Maria Remarque's *Im Westen nichs Neues* as *All Quiet on the Western Front* (which sold 250,000 copies in its first year), Robert Graves's *Goodbye to All That* and Richard Aldington's *Death of a Hero*.

Many of these books – though by no means all of them – were harshly critical of the war, portraying it through disenchanted, and, in the more extreme instances, disillusioned eyes as needless waste and hopeless sacrifice. At the same time a steady stream of titles with a positive view of the war continued to appear, and these maintained strong sales – not surprisingly, as they offered far greater consolation for bereavement and loss than the books that represented the war as futile. In some more ambiguous cases, the question of whether or not a memoir, novel or play was 'anti-war' lay very much in the eye of the beholder. The most obvious example of this was Sherriff's *Journey's End*, which quickly acquired a reputation as an anti-war play, even though Sherriff himself insisted that it was nothing of the kind and that he was simply telling the facts as he had seen them, based on his experience of the trenches as a captain in the 9th East Surrey regiment.

To an extent that's now almost impossible to gauge, there is also some truth in the idea that the public's appetite for the disillusioned picture of the war was a product not of the war itself, but of a more general disillusionment with the condition of Britain at the end of the 1920s. Widespread expectations of post-war prosperity – 'a land fit for heroes' – had been sorely disappointed, and, following the Wall Street crash at the end of 1929, a new era beckoned for Britain of even higher unemployment and lines of hunger marchers.

The war books boom soon turned into a war books controversy, as critics and commentators fought entrenched battles in the press over the issue of whether the disillusioned look back at the war, with its image of doomed youth led blindly to slaughter by incompetent generals, 'without their deaths helping any cause or doing any good', owed rather more to the reconstruction of memory than to actual experience. There was hotly contested debate about the predilection of the disillusioned school for scenes of horror, brutality and bloodlust, and questions about just how representative these were of what most fighting men had gone through. There were reminders that, while war had been hell, it had been hell with some worthwhile purpose. And there were dire warnings about the risks for the future of portraying war as such undiluted horror (the British Army was said to be seriously worried about the effect that *Journey's End* might have on recruitment).

Following these debates closely, Vera had her own contribution to make. Where in any of these books by men was there to be found an adequate account of the wartime experiences of women? She launched a fierce attack on Richard Aldington, in a review of his *Death of a Hero*, in November 1929, for the 'cynical fury of scorn' he had directed at the wartime suffering of women; and then, in a series of articles, proceeded to make more general criticisms of the belittling and insulting portrayal of women in the current spate of war literature. Either women didn't appear in these books at all, or they were depicted as passive, sentimentalised creatures, 'giving their husbands and sons and weeping unavailing tears, or worse still, as time-servers, parasites or prostitutes.' Furthermore, these books failed to give acknowledgement to women's active role in the war. The story of the women who worked on the land, or in munitions factories, of the WAACs, the WRAFs and the WRENs, and of the trained or volunteer nurses, existed only as dry statistics in the pages of government reports. Who, she asked, would write their epic of the war?

Vera made no 'puerile claim' to the equality of women's suffering and service of wartime with that of men; but she did argue that 'any picture of the War years is incomplete which omits those aspects that concern mainly women'. With the insularity of many of Roland's letters from Flanders and France perhaps in mind, she further claimed that a woman who had worked with the armies could provide 'a wider and more truthful picture of the war as a whole' than the soldier whose knowledge was inevitably 'confined to a small corner of the front.' This latter point was similar to one made by Mary Lee, American author of the novel, *It's a Great War* (1929). Lee had observed that civilians possessed a more comprehensive view of the war than its combatants – a remark that earned her a misogynistic put-down from the British military historian Cyril Falls. Falls wrote condescendingly that 'really, it is not the place of women to talk of mud ... [and Lee] is wholly mistaken in her notion that important books on the War must be written by women.'

Of course, many books by women about the war had already been published, both during the war years themselves and in the decade since. Mary Borden's *The Forbidden Zone*, for example, published in 1929 (though much of the book had been written during the war) was a compilation of sketches, short stories and poems, derived from Borden's nursing experience in a mobile hospital attached to the French Army at the Front. Borden claimed to have 'blurred the bare horror of facts and softened the reality in spite of myself'; but the deadpan manner in which she relates the mutilation of heads and limbs only adds to the reader's sense of revulsion, as a human knee is mistaken for a ragout of mutton, and half of the brain of a soldier comes off in a bandage and is placed in a pail under the operating table.

Vera had warm words of commendation for Mary Lee's *It's a Great War* as 'an immensely detailed and impressive book', while pointing out that, since the book was American, it dealt with the war only from 1917 onwards. Later, she would read, 'with deep interest and sympathy', Irene Rathbone's novel *We That Were Young* (1932), based on Rathbone's own experiences as a VAD, like Vera, at the First London General, and have words of praise for Ruth Holland's *The Lost Generation*, another novel published the same year. The missing generation of Holland's title refers not so much to the young men who at least had the advantage of having gone to their deaths with their illusions about the war partially intact, as to the survivors left behind, who find it difficult to rebuild their lives in an alien world where the younger generation simply wants to put the past and its sacrifices behind them.

Nevertheless, it remained true that, despite the growing list of war books by women, none of them to date had made an impact comparable to the most famous books about the war by men. Studying the works of Blunden, Sassoon and Graves with 'scientific precision', Vera reached the conclusion that her story was as interesting as theirs. 'I am reading "Undertones of War",' she wrote to Winifred at Christmas 1928; 'grave, dignified but perfectly simple and straightforward; why shouldn't I write one like that?'

The war book that Vera finally began to plan towards the end of 1929 would be an autobiography – or, as she called it, 'An Autobiographical Study of the years 1900–1925' – as well as the biography of her own generation of men and women: the so-called 'War Generation'. An auto-biography, with its assured first-person narrative voice (all Vera's novel versions had been in the third person) would rescue her from her none-too-convincing attempts to transpose real-life models into thinly disguised fictional characters. It would play to her strengths as a journalist, allowing her to adopt a more analytical approach where necessary. And it would greatly expand the range of the book, showing how Vera's post-war commitment to feminism and peace had evolved out of the experiences of her first 30 years. Aware of the continuing strength of the market for war books, although with understandable fears that this was on the verge of disappearing, Vera wanted hers to be 'as truthful as history', while recognising that it also needed to be 'as readable as fiction'.

It was an ambitious undertaking, requiring enormous energy and commitment. Even at this late stage, Vera considered making the challenge greater still by writing the book in two volumes, under the general title 'The War Generation'. The first book, covering the years to 1918, was to have been called 'A Tale that is Told', and was to have ended with an epilogue set on the Asiago Plateau, and at Louvencourt, with Vera's visits to Edward's and Roland's graves; the second, 'We Who Were Left', would have extended to 1930.

But she went ahead instead with the single volume. It was called 'Chronicle of Youth' until August 1931, when a reading of Robert Bridges's epic poem, *Testament of Beauty*, inspired Vera to settle on the title, *Testament of Youth*.

A book that – in one form or another – Vera had already invested so much time in, and for which she had such hopes, was never going to be easy to write. The difficulties would be magnified by tensions in other areas of Vera's life: in her domestic life, her marriage, and by the discovery, in early 1932, that Winifred Holtby was suffering from a serious illness of the kidneys, Bright's disease.

The confirmation of Vera's pregnancy at the end of 1929 had meant that she was able to do little actual writing of the book for several months. Initially she was too ill to work, and then, in the spring of 1930, the family underwent the upheaval of moving into a new and larger home, 19 Glebe Place, a tall, thin, Victorian house off the King's Road, in Chelsea, where the Catlins' daughter, Shirley Vivian, was born at the end of July.

Vera could use some of this time, though, in assembling her research, and in structuring the chapters. Looking up details of the past in old diaries and letters from the war, including her correspondence with Roland (Vera's side of which had been returned to her for safekeeping before his death), convinced her that these contemporary sources, historical records as well as personal materials, would give a special vibrancy to her narrative. She prepared 'scaffolding' for each chapter, copying out relevant extracts from her diary and letters – with stray recollections jotted down on tiny strips of paper as they came to mind – as well as a chronology of public events derived from the *Annual Register*, newspapers in the British Museum, and the collections of the British Red Cross Society and the Imperial War Museum (then still situated in Kensington).

One obstacle Vera was to face rather late in the day was the difficulty involved in quoting in print from letters written to her by Roland, Victor and Geoffrey. She was determined to quote freely from these, convinced that they would bring back, as nothing else could, the characters of her major protagonists. However, the discovery that the copyright belonged to the dead men's families threw her into a panic. She eventually preserved the anonymity of Victor and Geoffrey by putting them in the book without mentioning their surnames, and paraphrasing their letters to her to avoid any copyright problems (the copyright of Edward's letters, of course, belonged to Vera's parents and no problem would arise there). But she worried that the Leightons would never give her permission to use Roland's poems or his letters. Part of the trouble, Vera wrote, was that Mrs Leighton, 'though always very decent to me while R was alive, became very jealous of me after he was dead'. Furthermore, the Leightons were 'rampant Conservatives', 'patriotically militaristic', and had disapproved of Vera's political and feminist activities since the war. Clare Leighton, Roland's sister, insisted that Vera would have to remove her family's name altogether, '& only refer to them anonymously', and so it was to Vera's considerable surprise, after writing a flattering letter to Marie Leighton, that she received permission to publish not only Roland's poetry but also his letters.

In publishing Roland's love letters, Vera knew that she ran the risk, according to the standards of the time, of finding herself accused of 'bad taste', in telling the world 'a tale of private lives, private ambitions, private sorrows' (and this applied not only to the war sections of the book but also to her portrayal of her relationships with Winifred and with George in the final chapters). Yet, as Vera subsequently argued in the publicity material for the book:

> I don't believe we are entitled to keep to ourselves any jot or tittle of experience the knowledge of which can in any way assist our fellow mortals. A personal difficulty overcome, a grief survived, a philosophy evolved out of sorrow – these things are not ours; they belong to the collective effort of humanity.

> What really matters, for example, about a life like mine? It is that as many people as possible should know ... that this is the effect of war ... not that I should be able to say with smug satisfaction: this was my private life ... and I've kept it to myself.

By early 1931, after nursing the new baby for six months, Vera was writing *Testament of Youth* almost every day, in addition to contributing a regular column to the periodical, *The Nation*. Throughout the next two years she would continue to work in earnest on the book. Progress was sometimes halted by household crises, childcare problems, or by a sense of general discouragement – that the book was too long and that interest in books

An early typed draft of the opening page of the first chapter
of *Testament of Youth*.

about the war would have long since dissipated by the time she had finished it. Despite the advantage she enjoyed of considerable paid help with the children, Vera often felt overwhelmed by her responsibility for them, especially when they fell ill, feelings exacerbated by the fact that, during George Catlin's long absences from home while teaching in America, she was effectively a single parent. 'My "Testament of Youth",' she wrote with some exasperation to Winifred, in August 1931, 'if only … I get the time to do it properly, might be a great book. It is boiling in my mind and I shall become hysterical if I am prevented from getting down to it [for] very much longer … if I am to continue sane I *must* have … a) a rest from the children & the house and b) freedom & suitable circumstances to continue my book'.

Her sense of despair came to a head in early 1932. George had returned to Cornell after Christmas, when first John and then Vera caught chickenpox. At Oakwood Court, Mr Brittain was undergoing treatment for a serious bout of depression. Meanwhile there was cause for renewed concern for Winifred's health, as her illness was diagnosed as potentially serious, necessitating long periods of treatment in nursing and convalescent homes.

Vera badly missed Winifred's company, the stimulus she always gave to her writing, and the constructive criticism she made of her work. Deprived of Winifred's reassuring presence, Vera turned on a whim to a writer she barely knew. Phyllis Bentley, a Yorkshire woman of about Vera's age, was enjoying considerable critical acclaim for her novel *Inheritance*, which had been published by Victor Gollancz in March 1932. That spring, shortly after completing the Malta chapter of *Testament of Youth*, Vera set about initiating a friendship with her. She invited Bentley to stay in London – where Phyllis occupied Winifred's room at Glebe Place – threw a party for her, and generally behaved as if she was hoping that some of Bentley's celebrity would rub off on her, like literary gold-dust.

It was a disastrous decision, and their attempts at friendship ended in tears for the time being (in later years Vera and Phyllis would remain friendly acquaintances). There is no doubt that, while Vera admired Phyllis Bentley as a writer, she was deeply envious of her, too. As George Catlin acutely observed, Vera treated Phyllis like an obscure country cousin, and Phyllis retaliated by treating Vera as a negligible writer. From the vantage point of 30 years later, Phyllis Bentley wrote sympathetically in her autobiography, *'O Dreams, O Destinations'*, of the 'severe private tensions' on both sides that had led to the destruction of their friendship. She also commented on the 'prolonged strain' that Vera was experiencing at that time, as she tried to write her book through 'every kind of harassment and interruption', and admitted that '[s]uch a situation brings frustration to an almost unbearable pitch'. Phyllis Bentley's unpublished diary gives a much rawer picture of that frustration: of Vera declaring that her life was overshadowed by grief for Edward and Roland, and that only a great literary work could compensate her for the losses she had suffered in her life.

On 2 June 1932, Vera recorded in her diary the completion of Part II of *Testament of Youth*, which ended with her walking up Whitehall on the first Armistice Day. There were just three more chapters to go. 'It seems so strange', she wrote, 'that I have thought about little else but the War for eighteen years – and now, perhaps, shall never write of it again.' She had 'never shed a tear' over the parts of the book about the war, and was therefore surprised a few months later, while writing about her visit with Winifred to Edward's grave in 1921, to find herself so blinded with tears that she had momentarily to put down her pen and stop work.

For all the ill-feeling that by now existed between the two women, Phyllis Bentley did perform one notable professional service for Vera. In January 1933, when Vera had almost completed her manuscript, Phyllis, together with Winifred, persuaded her to send a copy of the unfinished book to Harold Latham of Macmillan in New York. Latham remembered 'a tiny woman with shining eyes' who dropped off a copy of the typescript at London's Brown's Hotel, where he was staying. Within a week, Latham had accepted the book for American publication, and this in turn encouraged Victor Gollancz, founder of the major British publishing house, to consider the book for his list.

Just before midnight on 16 February 1933, Vera wrote the final sentence of *Testament of Youth*. Five days later, she received the longed-for letter from Gollancz. 'I have read *Testament of Youth* with the greatest admiration', he wrote. 'It is a book of great beauty, and even greater courage, and I shall be very proud to publish it. In places, I confess, it moved me intolerably …'. Writing immediately to George with the news, Vera admitted that '[a]fter the discipline and anguish of a book that's taken nearly 3 years or more, I can hardly believe that the effort is nearly over'. And to Winifred, who was at her family home in Yorkshire at her father's deathbed, she sent flowers, 'with deepest love & eternal gratitude for believing in my book'.

There were still further obstacles to overcome before the book could go into print. For a start there was the protracted task of checking much of the factual detail. Obtaining permission to quote from poetry by various authors was another time-consuming process. Rudyard Kipling imposed an onerous list of conditions, involving five letters and two presentation copies of the finished book, to allow Vera to quote eight lines from his poem, 'The Dirge of Dead Sisters', describing the endurance of nurses in the South African War.

More unexpected, and much more disturbing, was George's response to his appearance in the final chapter, 'Another Stranger'. From Cornell, in April, he returned to Vera the typescript she had sent him with many of its pages scored out, and the words 'intolerable', 'horrible', 'pretty terrible' scrawled in the margins. He asked her to remove any references that might identify him, concerned that these might invite ridicule from his academic and political colleagues. He apologised if his demands appeared 'brutal', but added that 'just because it is a great book and yet also very personal to ourselves I don't want any part of it to be something over which I should squirm … inevitably the spotlight must come on me … but I beg that this spotlight pass quickly'.

To Vera this was an 'almost extinguishing blow'. She complained to Winifred that George wanted her 'to make him, in comparison with Roland & even with Victor, a complete cipher, & supply the reader with no reason whatever why I should decide to marry him.' She attempted to explain to George that 'my method throughout this book has been to illustrate the tragedies of Europe and the story of our generation by the fortuitous symbolism of the events in my own life; and my marriage to you, my resurrection from the spiritual death of the War … are absolutely *essential* as illustrating Europe's struggles after a similar new self …'. But it was all to no avail. With the publishers pressing her for the finished manuscript, Vera could not bear to contemplate 'a prolonged wrangle for weeks across the Atlantic', and so spent 'a miserable two days' removing the most obvious identifying detail, and also abbreviating his name to 'G.'.

With the book finally out of the way, at the end of July Vera, George and Winifred, in the company of their friend Violet Scott-James, took a brief holiday in northern France. Vera had resisted the temptation to revisit sites associated with her wartime experiences while working on *Testament of Youth*, lest they play tricks on her memory; but now she felt free to explore some of the places she had so recently described in her book. At Etaples, all that remained of the 24 General was a humped mound of earth, and, as she looked across the fields to where the German ward had once stood, Vera found it oddly disconcerting that it should now be so quiet and still, 'when I remembered it so full of hurry and anxiety, apprehension and pain'.

August · 664 pages · 8/6

VERA BRITTAIN'S

TESTAMENT OF YOUTH:

AN AUTOBIOGRAPHICAL STUDY
OF THE YEARS 1900-1925

Some advance opinions:

Sarah Gertrude Millin :

"It was my first impulse to write that 'Testament of Youth' is the loveliest book of its kind I know. But, really, it is the only book of its kind I know."

Phyllis Bentley :

"A particularly fascinating autobiography : a personal record of great beauty, insight and courage."

Storm Jameson :

"Its mere pressure on mind and senses makes it unforgettable."

Naomi Royde-Smith :

" I am still a little shaken by it."

Gollancz's catalogue announcement of the publication of *Testament of Youth* in August 1933.

In the countryside of the Somme, Vera returned to Roland's grave at Louvencourt, placing two withered roses – pink from the Leightons' garden and red from hers – against the words, 'Never Goodbye', on his tombstone. Afterwards they drove through Hédauville. Here, almost 18 years earlier, Roland had written his final poem about 'Another Stranger', and Vera was just able to identify '... the long white road/That ribboned down the hill'.

Testament of Youth. An Autobiographical Study of the Years 1900–1925 was published on 28 August. The reviews were overwhelmingly positive, and, in some cases, ecstatic. In the *Daily Mail*, Compton Mackenzie called it 'not merely profoundly moving ... but also extremely accurate'; Storm Jameson in the *Sunday Times*, under the heading 'Miss Brittain Speaks for Her Generation: War as a Woman Saw It', wrote that 'Its value as an experience and as literature, is above commendation'; while the critic in the *Times Literary Supplement* commented with approval that:

> In the important things of the story – tragic, noble, and in the end not without consolation – there is, in spite (or perhaps because) of its unshrinking frankness, no failure of taste, no irreverence or theatricality in the lifting of the veil from past sorrows.

That 'unshrinking frankness' unnerved the veteran critic, James Agate. He found the book's emotional candour difficult to stomach, and in one of the few adverse reviews wrote in the *Daily Express* that *Testament of Youth* was '[m]arred by a great fault – the inability to be content with the tragic and to refrain from fussing about it ...

The reader is affected as at the sight of a woman crying in the street.'

In the United States, where *Testament of Youth* was published in October, R. L. Duffus wrote eloquently in the *New York Times* that '[o]f all the personal narratives covering the World War period there can surely have been none more honest, more revealing … or more heartbreakingly beautiful than this of Vera Brittain's'.

Sales in Britain reflected this positive response. The first-day total of 3,000 copies sold exceeded the sales of Vera's five previous books. Within a week, the first impression of 5,000 copies had been exhausted, and by the middle of September 15,000 copies had been sold. It was to enjoy similar success in America where, on the publication day alone, 11,000 copies were purchased. In 12 impressions in Britain, up to the outbreak of the Second World War, *Testament of Youth* would sell 120,000 copies.

The book had struck an immediate chord with the reading public. As hundreds of letters poured into Glebe Place from men and women who saw their own experiences mirrored in the book, or who wrote that *Testament of Youth* had hardened their own opposition to war, Vera began to realise that the publication of this bestseller would change her own life. At not quite 40 years old, she had finally crossed her personal 'Rubicon' between 'unavailing obscurity and substantial achievement'.

She had also succeeded in erecting a lasting memorial to four young men, Roland, Edward, Victor and Geoffrey. She had exorcised the 'brutal, poignant, insistent memories' of her youth. Furthermore, she had ensured that a female dimension to the war was not forgotten.

Perhaps most importantly, she left a warning, which speaks to our own time as much as it did to the book's first readers in 1933, about the dangers of succumbing to the temptations offered by the glorification of war.

In her ideas for publicity, Vera had been keen to emphasise that *Testament of Youth* was far from being just another 'war book'. 'First and foremost', she wrote, it was 'a story of young love'. It was also, she went on to say, 'a tale' that should prove 'immensely interesting to all the women who are now coming into their own in politics and professions, of a girl's escape from provincial young ladyhood [and] of her experiences at Oxford both in war-time and afterwards …'.

In writing an autobiography set against the backdrop of the first 25 years of the twentieth century, Vera was well aware that she was making a contribution to the wider history of women's emancipation in Britain. Two chapters of almost a hundred pages precede the beginning of Vera's narrative of the war, describing her attempts to escape Buxton as well as her personal struggles for a university education. In her review of *Testament of Youth* in the *Daily Telegraph*, Rebecca West saw this section of the book as 'an interesting piece of social history, in its picture of the peculiarly unsatisfying position of women in England before the war'. And, in the three chapters that make up the final part of the book, following the granting of the vote to women over 30 in February 1918 – an event that passed unnoticed by Vera because of her absorption in her work as a VAD in France – *Testament of Youth* returns to feminist themes: to Vera's post-war involvement in equal rights feminism, to her working partnership with Winifred, and, finally, to her engagement to George Catlin and the promise of a marriage that will be defined in feminist terms.

Like other women who published autobiographies and biographical histories in the twenties and thirties – Beatrice Webb's *My Apprenticeship*, Ray Strachey's *The Cause* and Helena Swanwick's *I Have Been Young*, for example – Vera understood that the story of a woman's life could no longer be defined in terms of the purely personal. In light of the campaigns for the vote, and their experience of the war years, women could now see themselves as representative of the times, and their lives as a mirror of vast social change.

However, in fulfilment of this aim, *Testament of Youth* sometimes misrepresents aspects of Vera's early struggles for personal autonomy. Her description of getting to Oxford, for instance, overstates the single-mindedness of Vera's pursuit of that goal, while exaggerating her bleak isolation from the rest of the household (studying for her Somerville exam 'in a chilly little north-west room' with 'frozen hands and feet'). It ignores the considerable help, both practical and financial, that Vera had received from her parents – especially from her mother – so that Vera can portray herself as overcoming enormous odds to win a university education.

Most significantly, though, and particularly to readers coming to the book for the first time today, *Testament of Youth* stands as Vera's 'vehement protest against war'. While recognising war's 'moments of grandeur', Vera had wanted to show 'that war was not glamour or glory but abysmal grief and purposeless waste …'. This underlying theme of war's futility is expressed by the narrator's frequent foreshadowing of future events. So, in November 1914, Vera bids farewell to Edward, who is off to begin his training with the 10th Sherwood Foresters, at the entrance to Oxford's Little Clarendon Street, 'almost opposite', she adds, 'the place where the Oxford War Memorial was to be erected ten years afterwards, "In memory of those who fought and those who fell"'. Similarly, Vera tells us of the purchase of a 'black moiré and velvet hat trimmed with roses' that she 'was to be indescribably happy while wearing it, yet in the end to tear off the roses in a gesture of impotent despair'.

The beginning of the book also establishes the motif of a connection between war and celebration. As a child, noticing the banners flying to celebrate the relief of Ladysmith during the South African War, Vera is told that her father's brother, Uncle Frank, serving in the army, will be coming home. 'But Uncle Frank … never came home after all', Vera remarks, 'for he died of enteric in Ladysmith half an hour before the relief of the town'. This prefigures the death of Roland Leighton, some 15 years later, when Vera receives the news that he has been killed, during the celebrations for Christmas at the Grand Hotel in Brighton.

In a similar fashion, though this time for benign effect, the unhappy associations of wartime partings at railway stations are reversed in *Testament of Youth*'s final pages, when Vera is joyfully reunited with her fiancé 'G.' as he returns home on the Waterloo boat train to marry her. This was emblematic of a theme that was central to the book, as it had been to many of *Testament of Youth*'s fictional progenitors: Vera's desire to demonstrate that it was possible to overcome an overwhelming experience of loss and despair and renew one's life again.

A comparison between Vera's war diary and letters and her narrative of her war experiences in *Testament of Youth* reveals many disparities. In some respects, this is not surprising. Inevitably there are differences of content and emphasis resulting from the passage of time and the changed point of view of the writer. When Vera looked at the diary again, with a view to publishing it just before the Second World War, she could only discover 'a remote relationship' between her mature and younger selves. Her portrayal of her love affair with Roland is one instance of how the passage of time has smoothed away some of the stresses and strains that wartime brought to bear on their relationship in order to produce a picture of a more conventional romance.

But there are also more serious discrepancies to account for. The autobiography contains very little of the ambivalence towards the war – or of the bursts of jingoistic euphoria – that Vera had expressed in her contemporary records. The opening sentence of the book, explaining that 'the Great War … came to me not as a superlative tragedy, but as an interruption of the most exasperating kind to my personal plans', hardly tallies with her diary entries on the outbreak of war in which she is buoyed up by patriotic excitement, follows the international crisis closely, and echoes the bombastic rhetoric she reads in the press.

What Vera may conceivably be doing here is providing an illustration of how fatal it can be to the personal destinies of ordinary men and women to remain in ignorance of current events – a strong component of her journalism of the early thirties, where women, especially, are singled out for criticism for their political lethargy – but other differences between Vera's perspectives of 1914–18 and 1933 are starker still. In *Testament of Youth*, she reveals nothing of the part she had played, at the beginning of the war, in persuading Edward to volunteer, in determined opposition to their father's wishes. Was this simply too painful a memory to relive? This appears probable, but it is none the less regrettable that Vera is unwilling to explore the roots of her own idealism in 1914 in anything more than a superficial manner. She recoils from probing too deeply her own motivation, while, in the powerful 'Tawny Island' chapter, acknowledging in more general terms the susceptibility of her generation to the glamour of war:

The causes of war are always falsely represented; its honour is dishonest and its glory meretricious, but the challenge to spiritual endurance, the intense sharpening of all the senses, the vitalising consciousness of common peril for a common end, remain to allure those boys and girls who have just reached the age when love and friendship and adventure call more persistently than at any later time.

Although these anti-war views were without a doubt sincerely meant, there are parts of *Testament of Youth* in which one senses that Vera is fashioning her narrative to fit the prescriptions of the disillusionment school of war literature. One instance of this is her portrayal of Victor Richardson in his months at the Front before he was blinded and wounded, fatally as it turned out, at the Battle of Arras in 1917. Victor, as we have seen, enjoyed his life in the trenches, even to the extent of applying for a permanent career in the army. He had joked in one letter to Vera, at the end of October 1916, that he agreed with the Rifleman 'who when some dear old lady said "What a terrible War it is," replied "Yes … but better than no War".'

None of this is present in Vera's retrospective account. She downplays Victor's continuing support for the war – originating in his concern 'to prevent the repetition in England of what happened in Belgium in August 1914' – and portrays him instead, prior to his final battle, as full of unquestioning resignation to his fate, an attitude that he sums up in his final letter, through the words of the popular soldiers' song, 'We're here because We're here because We're here …'

Vera presents her own story in *Testament of Youth* as a 'fairly typical' one. But it is more precisely under-stood as a portrait of the war as experienced by the English middle classes, and by volunteer soldiers and volunteer nurses in particular. The book is also the classic exposition of the myth of the lost generation. The young men in Vera's story are representative of the subalterns who went straight from their public schools or Oxbridge, in the early part of the war, to the killing fields of Flanders and France. As a demographic class, these junior officers show mortality rates that are significantly higher than those of other officers, or of the army as a whole. Uppingham School, where Roland, Edward and Victor were educated, lost about one in five of every old boy that served. The Bishop of Malvern, dedicating the war memorial at another public school, Malvern College, observed that the loss of former pupils in the war 'can only be described as the wiping out of a generation'. The existence of a lost generation is not literally true, and is entirely unsupported by the statistical evidence; but, given the disproportionate death rate among junior officers, it is perhaps no wonder that Vera had come to believe, as she writes in *Testament of Youth*, that 'the finest flowers of English manhood had been plucked from a whole generation'.

The experience of nursing German prisoners of war, in the ward to which Vera was assigned for about five weeks on her arrival at Etaples in August 1917, was to play a pivotal role over the course of the next 20 years, first in the development of Vera's internationalism, and then, subsequently, her pacifism. The time she spent in the German ward provided her with the fundamental realisation that a dying man has no nationality.

It comes, therefore, as a considerable surprise to discover in examining the scrupulous records kept by the commanding officer of the 24 General that, contrary to the accounts in Vera's letters home in 1917, which describe the majority of her German patients as 'more or less dying', the statistics for the period show a very low mortality rate – in fact as low as 2 per cent among the prisoner-patients. How is one to account for this discrepancy?

There is little doubt that after the relative quiescence of her time as a VAD in Malta, where Vera rarely encountered patients who were seriously ill, the 'Active Service conditions' of the 24 General offered a marked, even a welcome, contrast; nor can it be disputed that, in all the pressure and excitement of those first weeks at Etaples, Vera initially exaggerated the plight of her German patients in her letters home to her mother.

When she came to write her account of Etaples in *Testament of Youth*, more than a decade later, this earlier exaggeration was allowed to colour the substance and tone of her description of the German ward. It should be added in extenuation that the parts of the book devoted to Vera's period as a VAD in France do not possess the reliability of precise chronology and detail of earlier chapters, for the simple reason that Vera had ceased to keep a diary on her return from Malta in April 1917, and had only some letters to her mother, a few rushed notes to Edward, and a sometimes hazy recollection of events that had taken place more than a decade and a half earlier. Her description, for example, of the British Army's only serious mutiny of the war, which took place at Etaples at the beginning of the second week of September 1917, is highly misleading. Not only does she place her account of the mutiny in October, she also maintains that she and other nurses were confined to their quarters in the first half of the month during the disturbances and their aftermath – a claim that hardly makes sense, given that, in September, during the actual period of the mutiny, Vera and her friends were allowed to move around Etaples and surrounding areas without any form of restraint.

Equally, though, there is no escaping the fact that the chilling power of Vera's largely fictional recreation of German prisoners dying in vast numbers fits appropriately with the overarching anti-war theme of *Testament of Youth*, and Vera's determination to prevent another generation from drifting towards war. 'I've been told that my book makes some people weep', she said, underlining her intention during the lecture tour of the United States that followed the American publication of the book, 'but I care much more that it should make them think.'

––––––––––

Testament of Youth was to have an unforeseen and far-reaching impact on Vera's life. At the time of its writing and publication, she was still some years away from declaring herself a pacifist. In 1933, as the final chapters of the book show, she continued to cling to the fading promise of an internationalist solution as represented by the League of Nations, with its ultimate sanction of the use of military force.

However, the process of writing the book undoubtedly hastened her eventual conversion to pacifism, which occurred at the beginning of 1937. For, looking back at the tumultuous events of her youth, she was able for the first time to separate her respect for the heroism and endurance of her fiancé, brother and friends from idealism about the war itself and the issue of what they had been fighting for.

Other factors were at work, too. Vera's celebrity as a bestselling writer on both sides of the Atlantic increased her public exposure, and gave her new platforms from which to disseminate her views. Amid the spirit of neo-pacifism that prevailed in Britain at the beginning of the thirties, Vera's readers now looked to her as 'a minor prophetess of peace'. The series of international crises of the early to mid-thirties, culminating in the subjugation of Abyssinia by Mussolini's forces, exposed the bankruptcy of the League of Nations as a voice for peace. Collective security – genuine internationalism of the kind that Vera had worked for since coming down from Oxford – seemed unattainable. Pacifism, and the refusal to sanction war under any circumstances, began to appear to some to be the only path that might guarantee peace in the long term. Personal tragedies may also have played some more indefinable role in pushing Vera towards a more radical affiliation. In the space of just two months, in 1935, Arthur Brittain committed suicide, and Winifred Holtby died of Bright's disease at the age of 37.

So when, in 1936, the charismatic figure of Canon Dick Sheppard asked Vera to become a signatory and sponsor of his new pacifist movement, the Peace Pledge Union, after some hesitation she agreed. Vera feared war even more than she feared the rise of Fascism in Europe. Ultimately, she felt that she should be one of the few who 'are needed to hold up before humanity the, as yet, but not always, unattainable ideal'.

She had not, as she once put it, become a pacifist 'for reasons of Christianity'; and, indeed, in the

two-and-a-half years that were left before the outbreak
of the Second World War, she devoted much of her
time to the search for political solutions that might avert
conflict. But, after September 1939, and, even more, with
the threat of invasion after the spring of 1940, Vera's
pacifism took on more of a religious hue. Its focus was
the maintenance of civilised values in wartime. Her
pacifism had a positive goal. In her fortnightly 'Letter
to Peace-Lovers', Vera insisted that pacifists had an
obligation to the community and to the society in which
they lived. She argued that, although they could play no
part in any activity which furthered the purposes of the
'war machine', pacifists had no right to remain resolutely
passive while the world around them was in such a state
of turmoil.

This meant in practice that Vera worked, at every
opportunity that presented itself, to relieve the suffering
of the victims of war. She campaigned hard for food
relief, to get supplies through to Britain's fallen allies who
were experiencing severe shortages because of Britain's
economic blockade of Germany and of all of occupied
and neutral Europe. And, most significantly, she was one
of the few who raised their voices to speak out against
the Allies' policy of the saturation bombing of German
cities, attempting to stir the 'uneasy' consciences of the
British people by making them face the truth of what
was being done in their name.

It was a courageous stand of conscience on her part,
and not without personal cost to Vera herself. She was
prevented by Government restrictions from travelling
to the United States to see her children, who had been

evacuated there, and consequently endured a separation from them for more than three years. And much of the American market for her books disappeared overnight when her protest against saturation bombing – called *Massacre by Bombing* in the United States, and *Seed of Chaos* in Britain – was published in the States in 1944.

She could never renounce her pacifism, Vera once said, because it was so deeply rooted in the first-hand experience of war that she had so movingly described in *Testament of Youth*: in the horror of nursing the wounded and dying; in witnessing the dreadful suffering that modern warfare can inflict; in losing the people that she loved most.

5   From Book to Film   1934–2014

The first plans for a big-screen adaptation of *Testament of Youth* were conceived 80 years ago.

In the spring of 1934, nine months after the book's publication, a Hollywood producer offered Vera $10,000 for the film rights. Elisabeth Bergner, the 'exquisitely *spiritual*' Austrian actress, was one casting suggestion to play Vera. Bergner had been a leading star of German theatre before moving to Britain following the Nazis' seizure of power and winning acclaim there, in film as well as theatre. 'She has your high forehead & delicate profile …', Winifred told Vera, '[h]er red hair could easily be darkened'. Vera was more concerned about how Hollywood might sentimentalise or distort the story. 'Of course a dignified, woman's Cavalcade film *could* be made of it, but would it, by America?'*

Could she ask the Leighton family to allow Roland to be portrayed on screen? And would George be able to

---

* The film of Noel Coward's play *Cavalcade*, which focused on the lives of a quintessential British family and their servants, beginning in 1900 and ending in 1933 (in the film version), had recently won the American Academy Award for Best Picture.

preserve any vestige of the anonymity for which he had fought so hard if the book became a film? '... Just think what Hollywood might do with "T. of Y."!' Vera wrote to Winifred. But the film plans came to nothing. While Vera hesitated, the offer was withdrawn.

In the late sixties, not long before her death, Vera made several attempts to interest television companies in *Testament of Youth*, encouraged by renewed television interest in the First World War. In 1966, Ernest Hemingway's bestselling novel from the end of the twenties, *A Farewell to Arms*, based on the author's wartime experiences of serving on the Italian Front, was dramatised by BBC Television. Two years later, R. H. Mottram's *The Spanish Farm Trilogy* (1924–6), a sequence of novels largely taken up with life behind the lines, and exploring the theme 'of what war does to civilised people', was also adapted by the BBC as a four-part television series (interestingly, Mottram had trained in Peterborough with the 4th Norfolks, in early 1915, with Roland Leighton as his platoon commander).

However, Vera's efforts were to no avail. She did believe that 'some day in the distant future when the First World War has really passed into history' a new type of interest would arise in *Testament of Youth*. But she would not live long enough to see it.

In November 1966, Vera was walking along Northumberland Avenue in central London on her way to give a talk at St Martin-in-the-Fields, when she stumbled in the dark and fell over some builders' rubble. Although considerably shaken and in pain, she fulfilled her speaking engagement, and only subsequently discovered that she had broken her left arm and the little finger of her right hand.

Her recovery was protracted and inconclusive. As the months passed, the mind that had once been so clear and resolute became clouded and uncertain, her memory faltered, and she dwelt for long periods in a silent world of her own. By early 1969, Vera was not only mentally confused but also physically very frail, and in January 1970 she entered a nursing home.

Vera Brittain died at 15 Oakfield Road, Wimbledon, early on Easter Sunday, 29 March 1970. She was 76 years old, and the cause of death was recorded as cerebral vascular disease.

In September that year, Vera's ashes were scattered on her brother Edward's grave at the small cemetery at Granezza, four thousand feet up on the Asiago Plateau in northern Italy.

───────────

Television's absence of enthusiasm for *Testament of Youth* was far from surprising. Throughout the course of the 1960s, as the First World War began to make an impact on popular history, the conflict was still viewed overwhelmingly as a masculine experience. This lack of acknowledgement of the wartime role of women was starkly demonstrated in 1964 – the fiftieth anniversary of the outbreak of war – when BBC Television's landmark documentary series, *The Great War*, devoted only minutes of its total running time of over seventeen hours to recounting women's experiences.

The fiftieth anniversary of the First World War brought recognition from *The Times* editor Sir William Haley (writing as Oliver Edwards), in a survey of the literature of the war, that *Testament of Youth* was 'the real war book of the women of England'. But it was none the less a further four years before the BBC attempted to interview Vera about her war experiences, and by then it was already too late. In August 1968, arrangements were made to film an interview with Vera at Whitehall Court, her London flat, for the BBC Two series 'Yesterday's Witness'. Although her powers of recollection were by then seriously impaired, it was hoped that she might rally sufficiently to talk about her nursing experiences. However, she sadly struggled to remember anything. In response to a question about Roland, she replied: 'Who is Roland?'

Slowly, the notion that war was man's business alone was being eroded. A shift in perspective away from the purely military sphere towards the beginnings of an understanding of how the First World War had affected wider aspects of British society – and women's lives in particular – stemmed from the work of feminist critics and historians in the 1970s. But it was also heralded by the more populist medium of television. In 1974, the fourth series of *Upstairs, Downstairs*, London Weekend Television's award-winning drama and ratings-winner – the superior progenitor of the twenty-first century's *Downton Abbey* – portrayed the impact of the war on the women of the Bellamy household at 165 Eaton Place, both above and below stairs. Three years later, the Imperial War Museum in London mounted a major exhibition, 'Women at War, 1914–18', which ran for seven months to record attendances.

The time seemed ripe for the reissue of *Testament of Youth*. A new feminist publishing house, Virago Press, with its distinctive apple logo, had been founded in Britain in 1973. Five years on, in 1978, Virago launched its Modern Classics list, dedicated to the rediscovery and celebration of women writers. At the same time, it began publishing a series of neglected non-fiction classics. *Testament of Youth* was to be among the first of these.

Carmen Callil, one of the company's founders, had been given a copy of the book by a member of Virago's advisory committee, Rosalind Delmar, and had taken it with her to read while on holiday in her native Australia. Sitting, reading it, on Melbourne's Elwood Beach, Callil was moved to tears, and returned to Britain determined to republish the book. In April 1978, *Testament of Youth* was reissued as a paperback under the Virago imprint, with an appropriately filial preface by Shirley Williams, at that time Secretary of State for Education in James Callaghan's Labour Government of 1976–9.* The simple cover design displayed the First World War's most iconic image, a red poppy of remembrance set against a sombre black background. (Virago's

---

* Gollancz, *Testament of Youth*'s original publisher, simultaneously republished the book in hardback.

Williams's preface made the claim, later corrected, that *Testament of Youth* was 'the only book about the First World War written by a woman', a prime indication of how forgotten and buried other women's accounts of the war were by the late seventies.

current critical edition of *Testament of Youth*, published in 2004, substituted for the poppy a picture of Vera Brittain in VAD uniform on the front cover, and placed a photograph of her war medals alongside a poppy on the back, to represent Vera's active participation in the war as well as her more passive role as one of the bereaved.)

Testament of Youth's reappearance was widely welcomed. Writing in the *Times Literary Supplement*, the novelist P. D. James recalled its original appearance as 'one of those books which help both form and define the mood of its time'. Many of the reviewers were at one in predicting that republication would find a new generation ready for the book, 'for', as one noted, it is a haunting autobiography that has no equal in World War I literature'. It quickly became one of Virago's biggest selling titles.

Not everyone was happy. At 80, living in the New Forest with his second wife, Delinda, Sir George Catlin (knighted by Harold Wilson for his work for Anglo-American relations) regretted the association of his late wife's name with a company trading under the 'deplorable title' of Virago. 'I have no interest in Viragos', he wrote with a sweep of his pen, adding that the name carried 'very misleading and damaging' implications. The precise nature of these damaging implications became clearer a little later, in a further salvo: 'I think it an extremely *bad* title (!!Lesbian)'. Recalling his battle, 45 years earlier, to ensure his anonymity in Vera's description of their epistolary courtship and first meeting, Sir George insisted that on no account was his name to appear in the publicity for the book, or in any of the introductory material.*

'What a magnificent series this book would make for BBC TV', ran an item in *The Bookseller*, in the wake of *Testament of Youth*'s republication. It would not be long before plans were afoot to bring Vera Brittain's autobiography to the small screen.

The enormously successful resurrection on television of *Testament of Youth* was largely due to the inspired efforts of five people, four of them women. Betty Willingale, script editor at the BBC, who specialised in finding suitable books for dramatisation on television, was determined that the project should go ahead. Jonathan Powell – the male interloper – a BBC producer, who numbered among his credits the recently acclaimed television adaptation of John le Carré's *Tinker, Tailor, Soldier, Spy*, was also very interested, becoming even more enthusiastic, according to one possibly apocryphal story, when he saw a rival producer reading the book at the Edinburgh Festival. (*Testament of Youth* was eventually co-produced with London Film Productions, the company founded by Sir Alexander Korda.)

Once the plans had received a green light from the BBC, Willingale sent a copy of the book to Elaine Morgan, the first choice to write the scripts, suggesting that an adaptation in five parts (of 55 minutes each) might

---

* He did subsequently relent and appeared with Shirley Williams in an item about *Testament of Youth* on BBC Radio Four's *Woman's Hour*. Sir George Catlin died, not long afterwards, in February 1979.

be a suitable length. Morgan, who had been writing television drama since the 1950s, knew of the book, but had never read it. In certain respects, she had some things in common with Vera Brittain: Morgan was a feminist and she had won an exhibition to read English at Oxford University's Lady Margaret Hall during the Second World War. But an identification between the two women should at once be qualified. Morgan's feminism expressed itself through work which overturned male-centred ideas of human evolution, while she arrived at Oxford from a small village in Pontypridd, where her father worked as a coal miner (after university Morgan returned to live in the Welsh valleys for the rest of her life).

Morgan remembered that in writing the five episodes, the first of which opened in Buxton in 1913, the length of the book and its rich and vivid detail were a great asset (drawing on years of experience, Morgan said that in scriptwriting it was much more difficult if the material was sparse and had to be filled in and expanded, especially if it dealt with real events where you were unable to invent additional episodes that might never have happened).

Two problems presented themselves at the outset. One was Vera Brittain's complete lack of humour, not necessarily the most compelling quality for a TV heroine, especially when it is essential to win audience sympathy for her. Morgan found Vera's complete honesty about herself to be something of a compensation for this, especially in the final episode where Vera admits to being 'horribly jealous' after Winifred's first novel is accepted by a publisher before hers. The other difficulty was how to convey the intensity of feeling present in the book simply by means of dialogue. Morgan recollected that it came as something of a breakthrough when she hit upon the idea of introducing voice-over quotations from the war poets – among them Rupert Brooke, Siegfried Sassoon and Wilfred Owen – at climactic points in the story.

Shirley Williams was very concerned with accuracy, although Elaine Morgan remembered her querying the wounded Edward's appearance at Vera's hospital after the Battle of the Somme in episode three, saying that this was simply too much of a coincidence. 'It had to be pointed out to her that there was no dramatic licence in this, and that it had actually happened!'

Moira Armstrong, among the first women directors in British television, was hired as director. She had read the book at school, where it had made a great impression on her, partly because her own father, at 16, had enlisted in the army during the First World War by giving a false age. Cast in the role of Vera was Cheryl Campbell, one of the leading stage and television actors of her generation, recently seen as Eileen, the schoolmistress turned prostitute in Dennis Potter's *Pennies from Heaven*, tossing her Pre-Raphaelite tresses over Bob Hoskins while doing a quick strip to the strains of 'Oh, You Nasty Man'.

The series was shot on studio sets designed by Sally Hulke, and on location at Buxton, Uppingham School, Oxford, London (filming the exterior of the former First London General Hospital in Camberwell), and Malta (not at St George's Bay, but at Mdina, the Città Vecchia,

Malta's old capital, which Vera Brittain had visited as a VAD).* Geoffrey Burgon's haunting title and incidental music – with its distant sound of 'bugles calling from sad shires', inspired by Wilfred Owen's 'Anthem for Doomed Youth' – captured the elegiac mood perfectly, and made a significant contribution to the finished programmes.

The first episode of *Testament of Youth* was broadcast on BBC Two on Sunday 4 November 1979; the final episode, five weeks later, on 2 December. The series was almost universally praised by critics and viewers alike. *The Times* thought that it stopped short 'only of the miraculous', while Clive James in the *Observer* marvelled at the writing, the directing and the acting, and wondered, tongue-in-cheek, whether it wasn't all part of a vast conspiracy on the part of the BBC to make Shirley Williams Prime Minister (Williams's successful BBC One talk show, *Shirley Williams in Conversation*, had just completed its run). The *Radio Times* received over a hundred letters in praise of *Testament of Youth*. 'We know that we have seen something approaching perfection', wrote two viewers from Cornwall; the programmes were 'wonderfully moving', according to Rachel L. Varcoe, who had gone up to Somerville as an undergraduate just after Vera Brittain and Winifred Holtby went down; a Glasgow man, describing himself as 'a combatant … in that war' could find 'no flaw in the action and settings for the period'. The series sent the book, in a new, mass market, edition published by Fontana in association

---

* A gazetteer of places associated with Vera Brittain and *Testament of Youth* can be found on page 222.

with Virago, back to the top of the bestseller lists for the second time in just under half a century (*Testament of Youth* would be broadcast in the United States, in November 1980, as part of PBS's 'Masterpiece Theatre' strand).

Shirley Williams, similarly, received a flood of letters about the television adaptation of her mother's work: from the war's survivors, now upwards of 80 years in age, and from a new generation of young men and women, far distant from the events of the war, who attested to the way in which Vera Brittain's story had moved and enthralled them. Among her letters was one from Maurice Richardson, Victor's younger brother. A retired school teacher of 80, living in Scotland, Maurice was the last surviving individual to have known Uppingham's 'Three Musketeers' well. His hero-worship of Edward Brittain as a recipient, like Victor, of the Military Cross, had led him in March 1918 to enlist in the Sherwood Foresters, although he arrived in France only days before the Armistice was signed. Maurice Richardson admired the BBC's *Testament of Youth*, but he singled out for criticism one scene in the first episode, in which Roland, Victor and Edward are shown playing cricket. None of the 'Three Musketeers', he said, had enjoyed sport, and Victor had had a special hatred for cricket (as another Uppingham pupil of roughly the same period, the artist C. R. W. Nevinson, testified, one way of escaping 'grim afternoons chasing a ball', in the sports-dominated atmosphere of the school, was to join the Corps).

For Shirley Williams, 'it was a strange and peculiar feeling, suddenly meeting your mother in the form of an actress'. She was highly impressed, though, by Cheryl Campbell's commitment to the role. 'She had really worked her way into the character in a manner I had not expected'. There was 'a defiant shyness about my mother which she fought to conquer, and Cheryl got that beautifully'. Cheryl Campbell received the British Academy of Film and Television Arts (BAFTA) and Broadcasting Press Guild awards as Best Actress of 1979. The series itself won the BAFTA award for Best Drama of the year.

Watching the BBC's *Testament of Youth* today – it finally made its way onto DVD in 2010 – the modern viewer may be struck by how dated the studio set-ups appear, or by the way in which the length of many of the scenes, with their high proportion of dialogue, gives the impression of filmed theatre. Fine acting from the actors playing Roland, Edward, Victor and Geoffrey cannot disguise the fact that they are in some cases too old for their parts, depriving the characters and their situations of some of their poignancy (the decision to cast older actors as the schoolboy subalterns was an inevitable result of having the 29-year-old Cheryl Campbell in the main role).

None the less, the intelligence of the writing – which avoids a slavish adaptation while successfully conveying the essence of the book – the beautifully judged, unobtrusive direction, and, most of all, Cheryl Campbell's luminous central performance, combine to make *Testament of Youth* one of the outstanding achievements of television drama from the golden age of public service broadcasting (which I would define, no doubt a mite controversially, as having started in the late sixties, expiring some time around the mid-nineties).

Ghostly soldiers, wearing steel Brodie helmets and dressed in muddy, blood-stained shreds of battledress, together with their spectral, sorrowing womenfolk in flimsy chiffon shrouds, dance to Francis Poulenc's hymn to the glory of God, against the background of a shell-holed First World War battlefield.

Gloria, a one-act ballet by Kenneth MacMillan, the leading ballet choreographer of his time, premièred at the Royal Opera House in Covent Garden in October 1980. MacMillan described it as 'a lament and thanksgiving to the generation that perished in the 1914–18 War'. Throughout his career, MacMillan had wanted to create a ballet that would portray the consequences of war and the anguish of loss. The spur that ultimately allowed him to do this was Vera Brittain's *Testament of Youth*. MacMillan had seen the BBC's dramatisation in 1979 and had turned to the book as a consequence. On the opening page of the first chapter he found a poem by Vera, 'The War Generation: Ave', written in 1932 as she worked on her autobiography, which he later described as the starting-point for his ballet:

In cities and in hamlets we were born,
And little towns behind the van of time;
A closing era mocked our guileless dawn
With jingles of a military rhyme.
But in that song we heard no warning chime,
Nor visualised in hours benign and sweet

The threatening woe that our adventurous feet
Would starkly meet.

Thus we began, amid the echoes blown
Across our childhood from an earlier war,
Too dim, too soon forgotten, to dethrone
Those dreams of happiness we thought secure;
While, imminent and fierce outside the door,
Watching a generation grow to flower,
The fate that held our youth within its power
Waited its hour.

The ballet has four principal characters: two soldiers and brothers-in-arms, and a pair of female companions, who represent the dual aspects of the central woman character – light hearted, and grieving. Writing about the 2014 Covent Garden production of *Gloria*, Rachel Beaumont observed that '[Vera] Brittain's story is clearly represented in MacMillan's choreography, through limpid *pas de deux* and an excoriating, intense *pas de trois*, where the central woman holds the two men close to her'.

What, though, is additionally fascinating about *Gloria* is the way in which *Testament of Youth* allowed Kenneth MacMillan to achieve his own personal catharsis. MacMillan's father, William, enlisted as a gunner with the Highland Fifth Garrison Artillery in 1915, and was caught in a mustard gas attack, a year later, at the Battle of the Somme, which left him with lifelong pulmonary problems and sores on his face and neck. William MacMillan died from pneumonia in 1946, when Kenneth was 16. Like so many veterans of the First World War, he had never spoken to his family about his experiences. Nor had he supported his son's desire to dance, and never saw him perform. Kenneth's first professional contract came at the same time as his father's death, and left him with overwhelming feelings of guilt that he had been 'unable to give my father the warmth he craved.'

Through *Testament of Youth*, Kenneth MacMillan discovered a way of expressing his anger at the horror of war and its devastation of his father's life, in addition to unlocking the guilt he had felt about his relationship with William MacMillan.

One of *Gloria*'s most memorable scenes comes at the moment during the *pas de trois* when the three soloists point accusingly at the audience in a gesture that clearly imitates Alfred Leete's famous enlistment poster from September 1914, depicting Lord Kitchener with his level-eyed frown and pointing finger. However, the gesture may also be interpreted in another way. Most of us, it may suggest, are guilty by implication in acquiescing in acts of war – out of ignorance, moral lethargy, or actual participation.

———

Flash forward to March 2014. It is the second week of filming on the Heyday-BBC Films production of the feature film version of *Testament of Youth* and I am standing stamping my feet in the freezing cold on a station platform at the Keighley and Worth Valley Railway in West Yorkshire. This heritage railway's fleet of steam locomotives and other rolling stock are being prepared for their first big entrance: a scene at Leicester station, almost exactly a hundred years earlier in the autumn of 1914, during which Vera learns from Roland that he will not after all be going up to Oxford for the new term, having chosen instead to enlist as a second lieutenant in the 4th Norfolks. As Vera receives the news in horrified disbelief – accompanied by recognition of Roland's excitement at the prospect of doing his duty in a great cause – they exchange their first, long-awaited kiss.

The railway carriages, normally kept in pristine condition, have been artificially weathered to remove their museum finish with a combination of black water-based paint mixed with wallpaper paste and vegetable oil. The station itself has been given new period signs and all the modern fittings have been removed; a cosy buffet has been created on the over-bridge between platforms three and four; and a newsstand bearing papers proclaiming ominous war headlines has appeared, although it will be in shot for no more than a couple of seconds. Later in the week, Keighley station – the location for the famous 1970 film adaptation of E. Nesbit's *The Railway Children* – will graduate to a bigger role, playing a major mainline city interchange, London's Charing Cross station, an illusion created with the help of architectural visual effects that will be superimposed during post-production.

Nominally, I'm present as Vera Brittain's biographer (my book has been optioned for the film), as one of her literary executors and as consultant on the production – although in practice being a consultant while filming is taking place means standing around on set hoping someone will ask you a question. To observe a feature film being made, even a film with a relatively small

(From left to right) Juliette Towhidi, James Kent, and Rosie Alison on the set of *Testament of Youth*, 2014.

budget like this one, is to marvel at the extent and smooth operation of the collaborative enterprise: of everyone – from camera operators to set dressers to the woman credited as 'Vera's hand double' – working together like a small, well-drilled army.

Only the extras, of whom there are around 50 today, seem somehow a breed apart. They talk familiarly among themselves, but appear to be overlooked by everyone else until the moment when the assistant director shouts instructions to position them. Wardrobe has costumed them, with minute attention to detail, as station guards and porters, as young Tommies carrying heavy packs, trying to look at ease in their puttees, or simply as members of the travelling public. A man wearing a neat trilby and a loo brush moustache brings the only animal extra, his dog, in tow.

The two principals appear unobtrusively on the platform: Alicia Vikander, 25 and from Gothenburg, Sweden, with her extraordinary command of English, as Vera; and Kit Harington, 27, as Roland Leighton. Widespread attention is fixed on Kit Harington's physical transformation. Contractually forbidden from cutting his long, tightly curled hair, essential for his role as Jon Snow in the long-running HBO series, *Game of Thrones*, Harington has been fitted with a £3,000 wig that miraculously hides his bushy locks and gives him a short, stylish cut with just the hint of a widow's peak at the hairline.

'You are always very correctly dressed when I find you, and usually somewhere near a railway station', Roland wrote to Vera in December 1915, shortly before the much-anticipated Christmas leave that tragically failed to materialise.

Vera Brittain's lifelong love of clothes is illustrated, not only in the many references to what she is wearing in *Testament of Youth* – a favoured dark blue silk dress, the black moiré and velvet hat trimmed with red roses, a dove-coloured coat-frock and terracotta hat, to single out just a few – but also by a letter she wrote to *The Times* in 1955, taking exception, at the age of 62, to an article on clothes for the older woman. 'I am not in the least interested in long sleeves, "sensible" shoes and "substantial" underwear,' she wrote testily, 'and do not expect to be for quite 15 years.'

Vera Brittain's interest in fashion is a godsend for the film's costume designer Consolata Boyle, though the character's appearance in almost every one of the film's two hundred-odd scenes has created a heavy workload for her, and for her team. In spite of this, Boyle, whose recent work includes costuming Meryl Streep as Margaret Thatcher for *The Iron Lady*, exudes an incredible calm, always dressed in black and moving about noiselessly, as if on castors. She says that whether she is designing for a period or a contemporary film she treats every story in the same way: 'creating a complete world that has to be visually coherent'. Vera's costumes include the fussy provincial apparel that strikes such a contrast with the dowdy clothes worn by the other Somerville students; the fitted coats and berets, like the brown coat and crimson hat that Alicia Vikander wears at Keighley today; and, of course, the heavily starched cotton apron and Red Cross badge of her VAD uniform.

On the second day of the Keighley shoot, I stand on the station platform with Rosie Alison from Heyday Films, one of the producers and the individual most responsible for bringing *Testament of Youth* to the screen.

As we watch the director James Kent, with his director of photography Rob Hardy, preparing for the next scene, she explains the influence of David Lean's 1945 classic *Brief Encounter* on the new film. It is not just the backdrop of the railway station that is common in different ways to both films, and the love stories that are central to them, but also the way in which the Lean film slowly builds the mounting intensity of Laura's and Alec's romance through chance meetings and the couple's brief interactions. 'In a way it's not unlike Vera and Roland', Alison remarks. 'All those poignant station farewells, enforced separations and snatched meetings.'

At that moment there is a shout of 'Action!' House music is being played over the loudspeakers to enliven the crowd of extras, as departing soldiers wave from train windows and couples kiss good-bye, clinging desperately to one another. As the train disappears from view with a hiss of steam, only women are left on the platform – mothers, sisters, wives, fiancées – 'frozen like statues in their emotion' in the haunting words of Juliette Towhidi's script.

At the end of the filming day, I cross over to a twenty-first-century platform to catch a modern diesel train back to Leeds en route for London, taking with me an unexpected residue of the steam age, dirt in the nostrils and under the nails.

The ultimate goal of Vera Brittain's literary estate had always been to see a feature film made of *Testament of Youth*. By the late nineties, I was one of Brittain's literary executors – 'like being the author's representative on earth', as someone not inaccurately put it – but, although TV companies expressed vague interest in the book from time to time, the film world seemed generally more wary of embarking on a potentially expensive period drama with what one executive termed 'a pretty depressing story'. Shirley Williams, a trustee of her mother's estate, felt strongly that the high benchmark set by the 1979 television series made another TV adaptation of the book unnecessary, even undesirable; and the notion that BBC television drama – certainly classic drama – had somehow lost its way was later confirmed for us by the BBC's adaptation of Winifred Holtby's novel *South Riding*, in 2011, where, despite an outstanding cast, the plot was unhappily truncated and the overarching theme of the workings of local government hopelessly lost.

Meanwhile, the publication and republication of books by and about Vera Brittain had started to prolif-erate. Biographies appeared, including the authorised life, based on the vast archive of her papers, extending to over 150 linear feet, sold to McMaster University in Ontario in 1971. Brittain's First World War diary was finally published in 1981, in an edition by Alan Bishop, while the letters between Vera, Roland, Edward, Victor and Geoffrey, from which Vera had been unable to quote freely in *Testament of Youth*, appeared in 1998 as *Letters from a Lost Generation*.

Both diary and letters highlighted the complexity and ambivalence underlying Vera's contemporary responses to the war. They revealed that, while at times she could rail against the war in anger and distress, at others she took refuge in a consolatory rhetoric rooted in traditional values of patriotism, sacrifice and idealism of a kind espoused by the wartime propaganda of Church and State, or the sonnets of Rupert Brooke. I adapted the letters for 15 quarter-hour, episodes on BBC Radio Four in October and November 1998, as part of the commemorations of the 80th anniversary of the Armistice. Amanda Root took the part of Vera, Rupert Graves was Roland and Jonathan Firth, Edward.

Ten years later, a BBC drama-documentary entitled *Vera Brittain: A Woman in Love and War*, based on the letters, and broadcast on BBC One on Remembrance Sunday, 90 years after the signing of the Armistice, brought *Testament of Youth* to the attention of BBC Films, the feature film-making arm of the BBC. Joe Oppenheimer, BBC Films' commissioning editor, was keen to press ahead with a big-screen version of the book. From the outset he stipulated that the story had to be made accessible for a new generation. 'It mustn't feel as though someone is blowing the dust off something from the past.'

I knew enough about the unpredictable ways of film to realise that there was still a strong possibility that *Testament of Youth* might never be made. I had read John Fowles's diary account of his 12-year wait for the film version of *The French Lieutenant's Woman*, in which you get a palpable sense of his steadily collapsing optimism and its replacement with an unmistakable form of writer's ennui. And then there was the dispiriting tale, which became common knowledge, of the attempts to turn Sebastian Faulks's World War One blockbuster *Birdsong* into a film. That enterprise seemed to have entered a special circle of development hell (the book was later adapted for stage and television, and may yet make it to cinema screens). 'The actress who will play Vera is probably still at drama school', we were warned as we signed the option contract. Other, more Cassandra-like voices cautioned, only half-jokingly, that she might not yet be born.

Nevertheless, searching for a co-producer, BBC Films met with an immediate stroke of luck. In the summer of 2009, Heyday Films, makers of the *Harry Potter* franchise, approached the BBC to express their enthusiasm for joining them in developing the film. Rosie Alison, who had worked as a director in television, including stints at the BBC's Music and Arts department and on the *South Bank Show*, before joining Heyday as Head of Development in 2001, had been 'spellbound' by the TV series of *Testament of Youth*, which she saw while at boarding school. Reading the book, she was especially struck by the 'psychological intimacy' of the author's voice, and the way in which Vera Brittain's 'fierce intelligence keeps digging away at the truth'.

At a lunch at the House of Lords, where Shirley Williams is a Liberal Democrat working peer, to celebrate Heyday's involvement, we debated the shape of the story, where it would start and where it would end, while Shirley Williams regaled the assembled company with anecdotes about her mother.

I sat next to David Heyman, the founder of Heyday, who, as producer of all eight instalments of *Harry Potter*, has become one of the most powerful and influential figures in the film world. We happened to have been at school together in London in the seventies. Heyman seemed very affable and charming (one prerequisite, I suppose, of being a good producer) and so I told him the only recollection I had of him from his schooldays. Our school buildings were situated around a large yard, and, as the teenage Heyman used to walk across it, other boys would push up the sash windows, lean out, and shout 'Hey! Man!'

This, I assured David Heyman, was because he had had the reputation of being one of the coolest boys in the school. He looked very pleased – as well he might.

The major problems involved in compressing such a long book to fit the confines of a two-hour film were obvious from the start. One casualty of this need to find a tighter focus was Vera Brittain's Malta experience, excised from the plot line even before the ink was dry on the contract. Everyone regretted that Malta had to go. Scenes of the sunlit island offered such a contrast of visual repose from those set on the Western Front. But in narrative terms Malta is little more than a diversion from the main path, and it had to be dispensed with.

I knew the story so well, and had sometimes dreamily imagined myself as an auteur, directing, writing and producing my own film of *Testament of Youth*, in which the predominant colour in my photographic palette would be a shade of red approximating to the colour of a faded poppy or of dried blood. Early on I wrote a treatment for BBC Films, utterly failing to recognise that screenwriting is a special art, not to be undertaken by any species of unqualified writer.

My treatment, I thought, started off rather well:

'The world was mad and we were all victims …'
An intelligent young woman from a sheltered background confronts the cataclysm of the First World War, as a nurse in military hospitals in London and abroad, and through the loss of the four young men she loves. The only survivor of her intimate circle of friends, she emerges into the post-war world determined to work for peace, and to ensure that the sacrifice of her generation has not been in vain.

September 1921. Northern France. A small car pitches its way uncertainly through churned up ground. As the shot widens, a shattered, shell-wracked landscape comes into view. The remains of trees, with bare, skeletal branches, assume grotesque shapes, while the humped ruins of houses line the roadsides. Here and there in the piles of debris are small groups of wooden crosses. Men and women, Army Officers and Women's Auxiliary Corps members, work amongst the smouldering wreckage, attempting to bring some order to the chaos.

The car's passengers are VERA BRITTAIN and WINIFRED HOLTBY. The two friends present a marked physical and temperamental contrast to each another. VERA is 27, small, dark and intense, dressed in high fashion in black, with her hat pulled down over her eyes. WINIFRED, at 23, is tall, blonde and gangling, with an exuberant personality and a more eccentric and colourful dress sense. Observing VERA'S pent-up state, she leans over and squeezes her gloved hand.

The car reaches the tiny village of Louvencourt, driving past a grey château, which immediately seizes

VERA'S attention. At the intersection of two roads on the outskirts of the village, the car drives up to a small military cemetery. It is one of the first of three cemeteries to have been completed in the immediate aftermath of the Great War. VERA walks along the paved path, and stands transfixed in front of one of the gravestones. She feels the incongruity of the cemetery's smooth velvet lawn when set against the desolation and disorder of the battlefields. WINIFRED stands a few paces behind her. She has no war dead, but has reverently adopted VERA'S as her own.

With a mixture of incomprehension and distress, VERA turns suddenly to WINIFRED, and exclaims, 'I can't feel that he's really here.'

And then a flashback to pre-war Buxton, spring of 1914, and Vera's meeting with Roland Leighton.

But as my outline proceeded, I became increasingly immersed in the trees and completely unable to see the wood. My knowledge of the minutiae of real events in Vera Brittain's life made me resentful of the need to abbreviate, or, worse still, radically alter anything. Consequently, my film of *Testament of Youth* would have run in its uncut version for about seven hours. As Joe Oppenheimer says, it is a bit like the story of the director who insists on cutting his own trailer and ends up with a 20-minute promo for his film.

Juliette Towhidi, chosen as the screenwriter for *Testament of Youth*, points out that one of the main pitfalls of the conventional biopic is to try to include too detailed a narrative of the life, which will end up making the finished film feel far too episodic. Towhidi, who had a major success in 2003 with *Calendar Girls*, completed her first draft of the script of *Testament of Youth* in the summer of 2010, after six months of thorough research and writing. Three further drafts followed, with more minor revisions and polishes. Towhidi was drawn to the 'very strong female voice' of the book, but saw that it was essential, because of its length, to identify the essence of the story and 'the emotional crest of the waves'. All the same, she adds, 'you have a moral responsibility to the characters to be faithful to them, even at points where, owing to the limitations of the time available, some streamlining is necessary'. In the 2015 *Testament of Youth*, for example, Edward arrives not at his sister's First London General in Camberwell, but at the hospital where Vera is nursing at Etaples. Purists who raise objections to this alteration might like to note that Vera herself moved the hospitalisation of the character of the wounded brother from London to Malta in one of her early fictional versions of her war experiences.

Towhidi came to understand *Testament of Youth* in certain respects as an intensified version of what we will all go through in the course of our lives: the devastating loss of people close to us and the need for us to rebuild our lives without them. 'Vera walks through the valley of the shadow of death,' Towhidi says, 'and one of the book's themes is the process she goes through to remake herself in the face of such terrible catastrophe'.

'You distil the story into something quintessential', Rosie Alison agrees. 'The book has its golden afternoon, climaxing in that final summer idyll before the war at the Uppingham Speech Day, in July 1914. Then it has the passing of a long shadow during the war years themselves; and finally, in the last act, the rebirth.'

'Making a film is a bit like childbirth', Rosie Alison observes. 'While you're going through it you feel as if you'll never want to do it again.' There are so many 'ifs and buts': finding the right cast, 'wooing' directors, avoiding scheduling conflicts and juggling availability to ensure that everyone is available at the same time; and then there is the incredible uphill struggle of securing the budget.

By the middle of 2013, four years into development, some of these elements were in place. The Irish actress Saiorse Ronan was attached to the project to play Vera. A British director, James Kent, was also on board. Kent is a seasoned, award-winning television director, and *Testament of Youth* would be his first feature film. Tentative plans were made to begin filming that autumn.

However, hopes for the planned starting date faded away as finance for the film began to look uncertain. Rosie Alison was working hard on Heyday's big budget, live action film, *Paddington*, based on Michael Bond's Paddington Bear books, but at the same time she and BBC Films were trying desperately to keep the prospects for *Testament of Youth* alive. 'In the end,' she says, 'despite all the uncertainty, the only thing to do was to say "we're making it" and move ahead.'

Using her own money to fund some of the pre-production costs, Alison hired the casting director, Lucy Bevan, and the designer, Jon Henson. She and James Kent started to research locations. One major find, straddling the borders of Nottinghamshire and Derbyshire, was the Welbeck Estate. Welbeck remains a working estate, but it also offers film-makers spectacular landscapes and a range of domestic and larger-scale buildings, many of them built by an eccentric Duke of Portland in the nineteenth century. Here the production designers of *Testament of Youth* would recreate the exteriors of Uppingham School, while Cuckney House, an attractive early eighteenth-century house, rebuilt and altered over the course of the next hundred years, would stand in for Melrose, the Brittain family's Buxton home. Woodlands on the estate provided ideal locations for the muddy landscapes of the Western Front, including Vera's hospital at Etaples. Other locations would include Brodsworth Hall, near Doncaster in South Yorkshire (as the Grand Hotel, Brighton); the Leeds City Varieties music hall (where Vera and Roland go to the theatre under the watchful eye of Aunt Belle); and the interior of the former Terry's chocolate factory in York (as the First London General Hospital). Merton, Trinity, Exeter and Balliol Colleges, as well as the city's glorious Radcliffe Square – brought to early twentieth-century life with horse-drawn carriages and vintage cars – would be among the sites filmed in Oxford.

Settling on March 2014 for the start of principal photography meant the unfortunate loss of Saiorse Ronan, the actress cast as Vera, because of her commitment to the film of Colm Tóibin's *Brooklyn*, scheduled to film at the same time. But *Testament of Youth*'s producers came up with an inspired replacement. The young Swedish actress, Alicia Vikander, had garnered rave notices for her English princess married to an insane Danish king in *A Royal Affair*, and for her troubled Katarina in *Pure*, and she was widely touted as a major new star with a line-up of future roles that included *The Man from U.N.C.L.E.* and *Tulip Fever*. She read Juliette Towhidi's script and immediately wanted to play Vera, encouraged by her father's conviction that she should take the role.

Kit Harington, whose outstanding performance as Albert in *War Horse* I had seen and admired at the National Theatre in 2008, was cast as Roland. He seemed able to convey just the right mixture of brooding pride and poetic feeling for the character. Colin Morgan, who later visited Blind Veterans UK (formerly St Dunstan's) in the course of his research, was to be Victor. The parts of Edward and Geoffrey went to Taron Egerton and Jonathan Bailey. A magnificent ensemble cast was assembled around them, including Dominic West, Emily Watson, Miranda Richardson, Anna Chancellor, Hayley Atwell and Joanna Scanlan.

BBC Films formally announced *Testament of Youth* on 4 February 2014. Seven weeks of filming would begin on 16 March. The week before filming started, Alicia Vikander was taken by Rosie Alison and myself to be introduced to Shirley Williams.

We sat in the tea room of the House of Lords, looking out across the Thames at St Thomas' Hospital, on the opposite side of the river, where Vera Brittain had nursed as a VAD briefly (and unhappily) towards the end of the war. Shirley Williams talked to Alicia about her impressions of her mother, her single-mindedness, her love of nature, her essential earnestness and complete absence of humour, and as she did so I could see that she was studying Alicia closely.

The only writer I've known whom I've seen portrayed on the screen is the novelist Iris Murdoch, in the 2001 film based on her husband John Bayley's memoir of her. (Actually I once met Philip Larkin and subsequently saw him portrayed on television in the guise of Hugh Bonneville, but my acquaintance with Larkin was so fleeting – and disastrous, as I accidentally knocked a glass of champagne over him, much to his fury – that it hardly counts.) For all her considerable gifts as an actress, though, Judi Dench bore little physical or temperamental resemblance to the Iris Murdoch I had met on several occasions in her final years. But for other filmgoers, who had never encountered the real Iris, Dench evidently succeeded in creating an illusion of the writer.

And that is what counts for most of us: that a film portrayal of a famous or well-known figure should create a convincing illusion. In the case of Vera Brittain, the actor's job is a lot easier. Few people are alive now who remember her. There are photographs, of course, but no movie footage (as far as we are aware). Sound recordings of her in middle age demonstrate that she had a fairly high-pitched, well-elocuted voice, not unlike Celia Johnson's in *Brief Encounter*. Any attempt to imitate this would produce a state of uncontrolled hilarity in a modern audience. So what one is asking of the actress chosen to play Vera Brittain is that she possess a passing resemblance to her, as Alicia Vikander does, and that nothing about her performance should jar with the information that readers have gained about her from her books. Everything else is about what sets great acting apart from mere imitation.

After tea, as we walked back along the corridors through the Lords, I could hear Shirley Williams wondering out loud about whether Alicia Vikander's nose looked much like her mother's. For a crazy split-second I imagined being in prosthetic nose territory, and a vision of Nicole Kidman's Virginia Woolf in *The Hours*, with her award-winning rhinoplasty, arose before my eyes. But, in fact, Shirley Williams pronounced herself altogether happy with the actress selected to play her mother, and gave her her seal of approval.

The director, James Kent, was frequently impressed during filming by Alicia Vikander's ability to sustain extreme emotion during long set-ups. At high points in the drama – Vera's reaction to the return of Roland's kit from the Front after his death, for instance, or to the death of a German prisoner of war in her ward at Etaples – a compelling flood of different, sometimes conflicting, emotions plays out across Vikander's face.

The idea of giving the film what James Kent calls 'an extremely first-person singular viewpoint', reflecting the autobiographical voice, was his strongest creative decision as director. The movement and positioning of the camera often represents Vera's point of view; while the journey from classically paced and measured camera work to something more chaotic in the film's latter half – hand-held camera, faster cuts and generally more movement – mirrors the dramatic and tragic twists and turns in the story, and sometimes Vera's own energy and forthright personality.

Kent was keen to strengthen the contrast between the 'idyllic pre-war story' and the horrifying conditions in the hospitals on the Western Front, which he believes were downplayed in the 1979 television version, where the depiction of Etaples was much more anodyne. The big-screen version of these scenes is like something out of Dante's *Inferno*. It has to be, Kent says, because the cinema audience won't be able to understand what motivates Vera to work for peace without first seeing the horrors of war that she witnessed at first hand. It is also inescapably true that members of the public today, in comparison with their forebears from the seventies, are much more conditioned by 24-hour news and documentary footage to extremes of wartime violence and bloodlust.

3 May 2014: the final day of filming, outside the Old Naval College in Greenwich, standing in for Whitehall on Armistice Day, 11 November 1918. As so often with film, it seems, the opening scene is being shot on the very last day.

It is a day of long and complicated set-ups, involving crane shots, crowds of extras, horse-drawn carriages, vintage cars and buses. The first minutes of the story, showing Vera isolated against a background of men, women and children celebrating the end of the war, are being photographed on film – as opposed to the high definition digital process used elsewhere – in order to give a dreamy, slow-motion effect to the images of the celebrations and Vera's response to them.

Listening on headphones to the soundtrack, while observing the action on a playback monitor, I suddenly hear the sound of a solitary mouth organ being played by one of the revellers on the street. It strikes me with a peculiar resonance. This, I realise later, is because it has reminded me of the ending of Lewis Milestone's film version of *All Quiet on the Western Front*, released in 1930, the first great anti-war film of the sound era. In its final scene, the young German soldier, Paul Bäumer, is sitting in a trench in a quiet period of no fighting when he sees a butterfly just ahead. A mouth organ plays in the background as Bäumer stretches out to the butterfly. He fails to reach it and then stands up to get closer. At that moment, a French sniper shoots and kills him. Bäumer's end, invented for the film and not present in Remarque's novel, is not dissimilar, though in a highly dramatic, romanticised way, to Roland Leighton's death by sniper fire in December 1915.

More than 80 years after its first publication, Vera Brittain's *Testament of Youth* forms an integral part of the way we view the British experience of the First World War. For Shirley Williams, hardly a day passes without someone mentioning her mother and how much the book has meant to them. In a way, the story of Vera Brittain, and her loss of the four men she loved, stands as proxy for all those of us, a century on, whose families lost loved ones in the First World War, and who want to derive some understanding of what they endured and suffered – as Kenneth MacMillan did when he choreographed his ballet *Gloria* to come to terms with his father's experiences on the Western Front. 'Others have born witness to the wastage, the pity and the heroism of modern war,' Winifred Holtby observed of *Testament of Youth* in 1933, 'none has yet so convincingly conveyed its grief.' It is a description that remains just as true today as it was when Winifred wrote it.

Shirley Williams is thankful for the 'precious kind of immortality' that her mother has achieved because of *Testament of Youth*, and she has high hopes for the new film version of the book, which will bring the story to a new generation, and to a wider audience than ever before, throughout the world.

In the summer of 2014, Williams visited Hamburg, in Germany, to see a section of the embankment in the Hammerbrook quarter of the city named in her mother's honour. Hammerbrook was a district that was almost totally destroyed in 1943 during the Allied bombing campaign that devastated Hamburg and killed more than forty thousand people.

Nearly a century after Vera Brittain nursed German prisoners of war in France, setting her on a path towards internationalism and eventually pacifism, and 70 years after she raised her voice in protest against the bombing of German civilians in the Second World War, this recognition from German citizens seems a very special one to Shirley Williams. 'It shows an understanding of my mother's contribution towards reconciliation and peace. And, ultimately, in a sense, it reveals the continuing power of *Testament of Youth*'.

Afterword

Ipplepen 269: The Tragic Fate of Edward Brittain

This short piece deals with the terrible circumstances of Edward Brittain's death in action in June 1918, on the Asiago Plateau in northern Italy. In addition to explaining how I came to write Vera Brittain's authorised biography – and all the difficulties and sensitivities associated with that task – it also describes how my research, together with a lucky coincidence, uncovered something of the truth about Edward's final days.

Despite this discovery, many questions concerning Edward's death remain unanswered. Vera Brittain, who learned about the mystery surrounding her brother's last hours in the immediate aftermath of Testament of Youth's *publication, inclined increasingly to the view that Edward might have placed himself deliberately in the line of fire in the battle in which he was killed, in order to avoid the disgrace of a court martial, while continuing to question the veracity of aspects of what his commanding officer had told her.*

Even at this distance in time, almost a century on from the events described, it should be possible to work out from sources like the battalion diary of the 11th Sherwood Foresters the identity of the other officer whose correspondence was intercepted. But I have never had the heart to do it.

Meanwhile, the story of Edward Brittain's sad end has recently entered fiction for a second time (the first was Vera Brittain's own use of the story in her 1936 novel Honourable Estate*). In Pat Barker's First World War novel* Toby's Room, *published in 2012, the death of the eponymous hero, serving on the Western Front, who kills himself in No Man's Land after being discovered having sex with a man, mirrors in its outline and many of its details the tragic fate of Edward Brittain in 1918.*

In the summer of 1986 I was almost broke and in desperate need of gainful employment. The previous year I had worked as a research assistant to the politician Shirley Williams, then President of the SDP. My main task had been gathering material for a book she was writing about the terrifying levels of rising unemployment in Thatcher's Britain. While Shirley dashed around the country addressing the party faithful, I sat in front of an early-model Macintosh in her London flat, unravelling, and typing, chapters from the handwritten scripts on long yellow notepads that she occasionally flung at me in her rush to the station. I also found myself inveigled into a fair amount of hoovering, and fetching-and-carrying of dry cleaning, though I rather appreciated the feminist role-reversal implicit in these activities. What I dreaded were my days at party headquarters in Cowley Street, avoiding the brooding Heathcliffian figure of Dr David Owen, the SDP's man of destiny, who was said to be

Edward Brittain's grave at the British military cemetery at Granezza, on the Asiago Plateau in northern Italy. A photograph taken by Vera Brittain in 1921.

more than a little concerned about the inefficiencies of Shirley's office.

But all this had come to an end with the publication of her book. It was called *A Job To Live* – an appropriate title in view of the situation in which I now found myself. For a while I drifted through an unsatisfactory series of temporary jobs. Then I hit on an idea that had been lodged in the back of my mind for some time: I would write a short book about Shirley's mother, Vera Brittain, feminist and pacifist, and author of the classic woman's memoir of the First World War, *Testament of Youth*.

I had read *Testament of Youth* several years earlier as an undergraduate at Oxford, and had immediately become obsessed with it. It opened my eyes to the suffering of the combatants and non-combatants of the Great War in a way that nothing else had, and made me understand the cataclysmic impact of the war on a young woman from an ordinary middle-class background not dissimilar to my own. It is also a book that is suffused, at least in its early sections, with the romance of Oxford, together with an excitement about the intellectual opportunities offered by the university, which at that time I certainly shared.

Another, more personal, reason for my interest was that two of my close friends, one from school, the other from university, were Vera Brittain's grandson and granddaughter. Some time later, after I'd been appointed as Brittain's biographer, I read Penelope Lively's fine novel, *According To Mark*, and relished the parallels in the plot to my own position in real life. Mark Lamming is writing the biography of Gilbert Strong, a literary figure between the wars, described as on the fringes of the Bloomsbury Group. In the course of his researches, Mark meets his subject's granddaughter, Carrie, and although he initially suffers from 'chronological irritation', because his version of events does not always accord with Carrie's memories of her grandfather, he soon falls in love with her, leading to momentous consequences for the writing of his book. I hadn't fallen in love with my subject's granddaughter, nor she with me, but I had experienced something of the same flicker of recognition that is present in the novel, when the biographer notices certain of Gilbert Strong's personality traits replicated in a later generation.

One of the bonuses of working for Shirley Williams was the chance, in odd moments free from all the frantic politicking, to talk to her about her mother, to look at old family photographs and at the William Rothenstein portrait of Brittain, painted at the height of the Second World War, at a time when her courageously defiant pacifist views were jeopardising her literary standing and isolating her from her friends. There were other, more poignant relics from the past lying around the flat. On the bookshelves, a first edition of *Testament of Youth* seemed to encapsulate the book's elegiac qualities. The Gollancz jacket was still bright mustard yellow, emblazoned with deep magenta lettering. Inside, affixed to the front flap, was a faded house photograph from Uppingham School, which included Vera Brittain's brother, her eventual fiancé, Roland Leighton, and another friend, Victor Richardson, among the ranks of the stiff-collared, dark-suited pupils. It had been taken in July 1914, and a note indicated that the book had once belonged to an

Uppingham schoolmaster. His inscription was touching and pathetic: 'I knew these boys'.

There was also the inky school copy of the Liddell and Scott, the Greek-English lexicon that had once belonged to Vera's adored younger brother Edward. Edward had left Uppingham in that fateful summer of 1914 and had responded eagerly to the call of King and Country, serving with distinction on the Western Front, before being posted to Italy where he was killed on the Asiago Plateau in the final months of the war.

Shirley was very supportive of my idea for a brief study of Vera Brittain that would set her life and writing in a proper historical context. At Oxford I had been awarded the history prize that, some 60 years earlier, Shirley's father, the political scientist George Catlin, had also won. Although she isn't a superstitious person, I think that this coincidence provided enough of an encouragement to her to believe that I was in some way meant to write about her mother. When she learned of my plan, Shirley immediately wrote to Carmen Callil, recommending both my prospective book and me. As one of the founders of Virago, Carmen had republished *Testament of Youth* in the late seventies with enormous flair and success, establishing the book, after a long period of neglect, as part of the canon of writing about the First World War, and pushing it once again to the top of the bestseller lists.

Carmen replied from her office at Chatto & Windus, where she had recently been appointed managing director. She wasn't keen on a short book, but she had another suggestion to put to Shirley: as the authorised biography of Vera Brittain by Brittain's friend and literary executor

Paul Berry was some years overdue, why didn't I step in as co-author to help him finish it?

I knew something about Paul Berry, and had met him briefly the previous summer. Born in 1919, the eighth of ten children of a Midlands farming family, he was a remote cousin on his mother's side of Vera Brittain's great friend, the Yorkshire novelist and reformer Winifred Holtby. Paul had introduced himself to Brittain at a Food Relief Rally in Trafalgar Square at which she was speaking in the summer of 1942. 'Charming young man', she noted in her diary, 'with a distant look of Winifred. He is in a bomb-disposal squad at Acton – [a] compromise bet.[ween] being a C.O. [conscientious objector] & being in the army'. On an impulse she invited him back to supper with her, and he stayed until after ten.

This was the beginning of a friendship that would last almost 28 years, right up to Brittain's death in March 1970. For Paul, it was undoubtedly the single most important relationship of his life. He was drawn to her, partly out of respect for his own mother whose 'sanctity and strong matriarchal influence' had, he claimed, made him a feminist; and also because he saw the vulnerability in Vera Brittain's character, perceiving under the rather flinty surface a sweeter and softer side to her personality that rarely emerged in public. This made him protective of her – in death as well as in life – and led him to imbue their relationship with an almost romantic aura. One of the first gifts he sent her was a box of violets, in direct imitation of those she had once received from her fiancé, Roland Leighton, fatally wounded at the front at Christmas 1915.

But it was far from being a one-sided friendship. Shy and withdrawn, Vera Brittain found intimacy difficult. At the time of first meeting Paul Berry, she was suffering from the devastating blow of being prevented by a government ban from visiting her son and daughter who had been evacuated to the United States. In Paul she discovered a young man who shared many of her views – he remained a lifelong pacifist – and who in some ways fulfilled the role of surrogate son. In 1944, when she was writing her novel *Born 1925*, she drew closely on his experiences as a bomb-disposal soldier for the character of the hero Adrian, who became a composite of Paul and Brittain's son, John.

For many years Paul had worked as a teacher of secretarial skills, eventually becoming a Senior Lecturer at Kingsway Princeton College for Further Education, from which he had retired in 1981. His major ambition, though, had always been to be a writer, and he had published two short books, one in collaboration with another author. But the book he most wanted to write had come close to defeating him. Originally intending, at Brittain's request, to complete her third volume of autobiography, left unfinished at her death, he subsequently conceived the idea of a memoir, and then, as Vera Brittain's reputation revived, of a fully-fledged biography. He had always experienced difficulty writing – though he was an accomplished and indefatigable correspondent – and found himself, understandably, floundering in the morass of material which Brittain had left behind, much of it preserved at McMaster University in Ontario, which had purchased the vast Brittain archive in 1971. 'It's the one thing I want to do before I go on my way – and do really well', he wrote to Carmen Callil, 'and it's soul-destroying finding it so terribly difficult.'

In the years to come, I often reflected on what seemed to me an extraordinary (though entirely characteristic) loyalty on Shirley's part towards Paul's overriding desire to be her mother's authorised biographer, often against a chorus of hostile voices from feminist academics in North America who resented the ban on the use of unpublished material while Paul was writing his book. Yet, as one of Shirley's oldest friends put it to me, a more complicated mixture of motives was probably involved. While she clearly felt a sense of obligation towards him, she may also have believed that she could rely on Paul to produce a respectful biography of her mother that wouldn't dwell on the more controversial aspects of Vera Brittain's private life: her 'semi-detached' marriage, ultimately a happy one, but for many years a source of conflict and estrangement; her great friendship with Winifred Holtby, for so long a subject of innuendo and rumour that portrayed it as a lesbian love affair; and, in her final years, Brittain's sadly deteriorating relationship with her son John. As I was soon to learn, another of Paul's problems was that he was constantly torn between his desire on the one hand to protect Brittain's reputation and on the other to be as honest as he could about her faults as well as her virtues.

Our first professional encounter at Chatto's offices in William IV Street was hardly auspicious. Having negotiated the tricky metal grille of the old-fashioned lift, I arrived in Carmen's room, its walls a virulent shade of yellow, to find her enquiring after Paul's cat, Bobbitt, and complaining about the state of the office lavatories. She was smoking furiously, and, as she turned her head, shafts of sunlight sent off rays of iridescent colour from her hair, Titian red, then rich aubergine. Paul regarded me with watery blue eyes, peeping over the folds of a large white handkerchief, a study in suspicion.

Carmen requested that he invite me to his home in West Sussex to look at the material he'd collected. When he demurred, citing the excuse of his large family and a sick friend, she suddenly transformed from benign autocrat to belligerent dictator: *he would cooperate and make everything available to me or else the book that meant so much to him might never appear.*

Paul had accumulated a massive Brittain archive of his own, housed in a cobwebby study at the top of one of the five tiny cottages that had been knocked together in a higgledy-piggledy fashion to construct a home. Here were hundreds of photocopies from McMaster, countless pages of Brittain manuscripts and news cuttings retrieved from her London flat after her death or subsequently donated to him, letters of reminiscence from people who had known Vera Brittain, and both sides of more than a quarter-of-a-century's correspondence between Paul and Brittain herself. Although I was to make trips to McMaster and to the Winifred Holtby Archive at Hull, as well as to many other collections, the discoveries that surprised me most were often those that I found under a pile of decaying newsprint on Paul's study floor.

It quickly became apparent that there was no book to finish, and that little of what Paul had written was usable. He possessed a striking turn of phrase, which I often adopted; but he was unable to see the wood for the trees, or to organise the material in a way that would produce a coherent narrative. Initially, his argument that we shouldn't write about Brittain's First World War experiences because they were so well known drove me to distraction. I would return from my visits to Sussex, my briefcase full to overflowing with files of fascinating material to work on, but with a sinking feeling about the prospect of ever being able to weld together our widely differing approaches to our subject.

With Paul himself I began to enjoy a real friendship, even though we were separated in age by more than 40 years. Our relationship was still tempered by his natural suspicion and stubbornness, and, on my part, by over-eagerness to probe deeply into every aspect of Vera Brittain's life and career. But I appreciated his inexhaustible generosity ('there are no pockets in the shrouds', he would say as he slipped me a £20 note) and recognised the quiet integrity that struck everyone who knew him. My visits to the picturesque little cottages with their lush surrounding garden, nestling by a river, became more frequent; but, as the years passed, our roles reversed. I was writing more and more, while he increasingly assumed an editorial responsibility, poring over my typescripts and scrutinising them for grammatical error, infelicities of expression and factual mistakes. I knew how desperate he was that the book should appear, but my progress was interrupted by my spells of employment at the BBC, when I barely had time to write at all. Today, reading the letters I wrote to

Paul during this period, I am filled with shame at their constant note of prevarication and delay. Year after year I promise him that the completion of the book is imminent. By the beginning of 1994, he was seriously ill and had begun to put real pressure on me: he might not live to see its publication. That summer I finally finished it, but working with a sympathetic copy editor persuaded me that it could be improved still further, and in the last four months of that year I drastically rewrote it. Paul couldn't disguise his anger. Although we were reconciled long before his death in 1999, there was always the unspoken accusation between us, that I had taken his book away from him. What he can't have failed to recognise is that he had given the biography something infinitely precious: that stamp of authenticity that can only come from close personal knowledge of the biographer's subject.

For more than 30 years Paul had shared his life with the distinguished potter Ray Marshall, and, after Marshall's death in 1986, he had spent his final decade in a happy companionship with the artist Eric Leazell. Paul wasn't tortured or defensive about his homosexuality, though he was secretive about it, understandably, given that he had grown to maturity in pre-Wolfenden days. And his sexuality had perhaps led him to examine in some detail the character of Vera Brittain's brother Edward, and the circumstances surrounding his death in 1918. On one of my first visits to see him, Paul had shown me the letters relating to this episode that he had uncovered at McMaster.

Edward is a tragic subsidiary character in Vera Brittain's story. He – along with his Uppingham friends, Roland Leighton and Victor Richardson – exemplified the volunteer spirit of the public schoolboys who rushed to enlist on the declaration of war in 1914. When Edward was gazetted to a battalion of the Sherwood Foresters, he proudly sent a photograph of himself in 'the King's uniform' to his old governess. 'What greater honour', she replied, 'could any man have at such a time as this in our history!'

Edward became a family hero, awarded the Military Cross 'for conspicuous gallantry and leadership during an attack' on the first day of the Battle of the Somme. However, the experience of crawling back in great pain to the safety of the British trenches through the dead and wounded, with corpses already turning yellow and green, had eroded his youthful idealism. 'You have no idea how bitter life is at times', he wrote to Vera when he was back in the mud and cold of the Ypres Salient.

By the autumn of 1917, when he was posted to Italy, he had suffered the deaths of his old friends, Roland and Victor, and of another close friend from his former battalion, Geoffrey Thurlow, all fatally wounded or killed on the Western Front, and these had intensified Edward's long-held premonition that he, too, would be killed. His family's hopes, though, that he would survive the war were boosted now that Edward was in the relatively quiescent Italian Front high in the Alps above Vicenza.

But those hopes were shattered on 22 June 1918 by the arrival of a telegram informing the Brittains that

Edward had been killed on the Asiago Plateau while leading a counter-offensive against an Austrian attack. The absence of any firm details about Edward's death led Vera Brittain to contact his commanding officer, who was in hospital in London recovering from the injuries he had sustained in the same battle. For several months she pursued him relentlessly, convinced that he knew far more about Edward's part in the action than he was prepared to tell. However, it was all to no avail, and Edward's final hours remained cloaked in mystery.

This much was recounted in *Testament of Youth* and confirmed by the contemporary documents. But the McMaster material added an intriguing new twist to the plot. In 1934, 15 years after Edward's death, and following the publication of *Testament of Youth*, the commanding officer had written to Vera, out of the blue, to confess that, as she had intuitively believed in 1918, he had withheld certain facts of a personal nature about Edward's death. Even at that distance in time he could not bring himself to write about it, but he suggested that if she still wished to have the information they could meet for a talk.

But what were these facts of a personal nature that the commanding officer couldn't write down? Here, tantalisingly, the written sources went blank. From subsequent letters among the Brittain papers, it was clear that a meeting had taken place, but of their conversation, no record appeared to survive.

Paul pointed to the evidence of Vera Brittain's third novel, an ambitious feminist epic, *Honourable Estate*, which Brittain had written after *Testament of Youth*, but which had failed to repeat the runaway success of her autobiography. The book had been published in 1936, a couple of years after the commanding officer had met for his conversation with Brittain. Each of Vera Brittain's five novels is a *roman à clef* in which identifiable persons from real life are presented as thinly disguised fictional characters; even so, the plotline of *Honourable Estate* seemed almost too dramatic to be true. In the novel, Richard Alleyndene, the brother of the heroine Ruth, goes into the Gallipoli campaign seeking to be killed in order to avoid a court martial for homosexuality. 'I can't confront Father and Mother with the fact that their son is what they would call vicious and immoral', he tells her in a farewell letter, 'instead of a virtuous patriotic hero'.

Staying at about this time with George Catlin's second wife, Delinda, who, since his death in 1979, had lived in Vera Brittain's cottage in the New Forest, I made a small but satisfying find. At the bottom of the bathroom cupboard, covered in thick dust, was a head and shoulders portrait of Edward, wearing his M.C. The canvas had holes in it and the paint was peeling, but I could make out his sad smile and dignified bearing. I took it downstairs to show Delinda, who was nursing her lunchtime gin and tonic.

Delinda was the consummate hostess, having in the distant past been the manager of several upmarket hotels. In every way imaginable I was the polar opposite of her distinguished predecessor, Vera Brittain, who had wasted no time on culinary matters, being barely able to boil an egg. Among other things, Delinda rejected books, feminism, the Labour Party, or anything else that smacked of intellectualism. She verbalised her thoughts in a down-to-earth, call-a-spade-a-spade fashion that emanated from her Newcastle-upon-Tyne roots. 'Dahling,' she drawled after taking one look at the painting, 'of course, everyone knows he was a pansy.'

Like Chinese whispers, other unsubstantiated rumours swirled around Edward's name. An academic researching the novelist Joyce Cary reported that Cary's brother-in-law, Heneage Ogilvy, who had been a surgeon at Asiago in 1918, had known something about a court martial in connection with Edward. But having been unable to gain access to the official records held by the Ministry of Defence, which at the time were embargoed, I tried to think of other leads to follow.

Another obvious starting point was Edward's commanding officer. In Richmond Reference Library, near where I lived, I located the entry for Brigadier C. E. Hudson, in the 1951–60 volume of *Who Was Who*. This revealed that Hudson had remained in the army after the war, becoming Chief Instructor at the Royal Military College at Sandhurst, and eventually, during the Second World War, A.D.C. to George VI. He had had one son, had died in 1959, and his address had been Denbury Manor in Devon. The book even helpfully gave his telephone number – Ipplepen 269 – though since he was dead that seemed, to put it mildly, somewhat superfluous.

Ipplepen 269. Over the next few weeks the number seared itself on my brain. I rang British Telecom on several occasions to see whether an operator could convert the number into its modern day equivalent, but, the harder I tried to explain what I was attempting to do, the more convoluted a muddle both the operator and I seemed to get into. Finally, I had almost decided to travel down to Devon to see if the house was still standing, when I had another idea. Hudson had been at Sherborne School. Wasn't there a chance that he might have sent his son there too? Feeling slightly fainthearted now, I rang the Sherborne Old Boys Association, spoke to its secretary, and explained my predicament. He was doubtful about any prospect of success, but promised to do what he could. A week later, having forgotten all about it, I was just sitting down to dinner when I received a call from the secretary. My guess had been right. Hudson had sent his son to Sherborne, and he gave me the son's telephone number.

I nervously rang the number. A woman answered, identifying herself as the son's wife. I embarked on my story, but she stopped me after several sentences. 'Good gracious', she said. 'We've been expecting someone to contact us about this for years.'

Hudson's son couldn't have been more open and helpful. As I struggled to contain my excitement, he told me that his father had recorded all that he knew about Edward's death in his unpublished memoirs and that, of course, I was welcome to read them. 'What a wonderful coup tracking down Hudson's son', Paul wrote to me when he heard the news. 'That really is *something*.' Looking at Paul's letter as I write this, I see that it is dated 15 June 1989, the 71st anniversary of Edward's death.

However, Hudson's son did make one proviso. I must first obtain Shirley Williams's permission before he could allow me to see the contents of his father's book. This proved to be much more of an obstacle than I anticipated.

Shirley had been remarkably generous in answering my enquiries, and in allowing me access to material in her possession. But in this one instance she at first expressed her outright refusal to co-operate. She wasn't at all sure that I should be allowed to delve further into the murky secrets of her uncle's past. Hudson's memoirs, she said, might only reveal Edward to have been involved in a love affair condemned by the bigotry and hypocrisy of the time; or they might show it be something discreditable, like the seduction of a young recruit by Edward as his junior officer.

I remember my feelings at the time as being ones of anger and frustration, during which I tried to enlist the support of other members of Vera Brittain's family to speak up for my cause. 'I'm really grieved and sad that you're having so much trouble from Shirley over the Hudson book', Paul wrote. 'We – and especially you – have far too much to do and worry about without this sort of spanner in the works … I'm sure you've thought of all the arguments you can use. I do hope that you can get [Hudson's son] on your side although I have a hunch that opposition only makes Shirley more determined.'

Looking back now, though, I see these events as much less clear-cut. As a biographer I had got hold of a good story which I wanted to milk for all its worth. It was as if I had been overcome by a kind of narrative greed, which paid no attention to the sensitivities of those more directly affected by possible revelations than I was. Much has been made of the ways in which a family can manipulate and bully an authorised biographer; too little has been said of the biographer's ruthlessness in sometimes wilfully ignoring the family's point of view.

In the event, it was Hudson's son who came to my rescue. He was surprised by Shirley's reaction, and had in any case only requested her permission as a courtesy to her. He was far more concerned with setting the record straight regarding the reputation of his father who, he believed, had been 'grossly traduced' by what Vera Brittain had written of him in *Testament of Youth*. After a couple of weeks, which I spent on tenterhooks, waiting for a final answer, we reached a compromise: Shirley would read the memoirs first in order to decide whether I should be allowed to see them.

So on a boiling hot July day, I made my way to Brooks' Club in St James's to meet Hudson's son. Twenty minutes before my arrival, Shirley had departed, after agreeing that I could read his father's book. In the staid, slightly incongruous atmosphere of a gentlemen's club, the shocking circumstances of Edward Brittain's death unfolded before my eyes.

On 12 June 1918, Edward's commanding officer, Colonel Hudson, had received a communication from the Provost Marshal, the head of the Military Police, informing him that a letter written by one of his officers, while on leave, to another officer in the battalion, had been intercepted and censored at the Base. The contents of this letter made it plain that the two officers were involved in homosexual relations with men in their company. The more senior of the two was Captain Brittain. Hudson was instructed that he was to avoid letting the officers concerned know that they were under investigation.

But, according to Hudson's later account, he was inclined to treat Edward more sympathetically, and on 14 June – the day before the Austrian offensive on the Asiago Plateau commenced – he had a conversation with Edward in which he gave him a warning. 'I did not realize that letters written out here were censored at the Base.' Edward turned white and made no comment. But it was clear that he had understood.

Edward was the only officer killed on 15 June. After the battle, Hudson had reached the terrible conclusion that, faced in all likelihood with the prospect of a court martial when they came out of the line, imprisonment and the subsequent disgrace that would ensue, Edward had either shot himself or deliberately courted death by presenting himself as an easy target for a sniper's bullet. There were some striking discrepancies in the reports of Edward's death: some described him as being shot by the enemy in full view of his men, others claimed that Edward had insisted on going ahead of the rest of his company, and that his body had only been discovered hours later, after the fighting was over, with a bullet through his head.

These disclosures, I knew from the McMaster letters, had understandably caused Vera Brittain some 'very distressful hours', though she had hastened to reassure Colonel Hudson that she did not believe that her brother would have taken his own life, or gone into battle seeking to be killed. Privately, though, she increasingly inclined to the opposite point of view, and dramatised the episode in her novel *Honourable Estate*. What was undeniable was that Edward's final days must have been very bitter. It seemed such a terrible end, to have survived almost the entire war, with the loss of all his closest friends, to have served his country with courage and distinction; and then to have gone to his death in circumstances that, at the very least, must have been unendurable.

After submitting my typescript of *Vera Brittain: A Life* to Chatto in the summer of 1994, I decided to visit Edward's grave at the British military cemetery at Granezza in Northern Italy, four thousand feet up in the mountains overlooking the Brenta Valley, on the highest corner of the Asiago Plateau. It was a fitting place at which to end my biographical journey. Almost a quarter of a century earlier, Shirley and her then husband, the philosopher Bernard Williams, accompanied by Paul Berry, had scattered Vera Brittain's ashes on her brother's grave. On my trip, Martin Taylor, a friend who worked at the Imperial War Museum in London, joined me. Martin had been extremely helpful in my researches into Vera Brittain's First World War experiences. He was especially interested in the sequence of events that had led to Edward's death as, several years earlier, he had edited and published *Lads*, a highly praised selection of the love poetry of the trenches. It is a moving anthology of the homoerotic verse of the war, revealing the affection between fighting men that often went beyond the bounds of ordinary comradeship. Shortly before we'd set off to Italy, Martin had told me that he was HIV-positive. At night, in the stifling heat of our hotel room in the town of Bassano del Grappa, I watched as he removed his shirt, revealing the horrifying purplish-black lesions on his skin. And I recognised the truth behind Martin's parting remark at the end of his introduction to *Lads*: 'Though we may not have lived through the nightmares of the Western Front, we now have nightmares of our own ...'. Edward Brittain had faced his nightmare, now Martin faced his. Two years later, Martin was dead, at 39.

We found the remains of the trenches, blown out of the rock, in which Edward and his company had spent their last hours before the battle, and then moved on to the grave. Raised sharply above the road, in a small natural amphitheatre, and surrounded by pinewoods climbing towards the skyline, the small cemetery contains the graves of 142 soldiers of the Great War, all of whom were killed during the decisive rout by British and Italian troops of the Austrian army in the summer of 1918.

Few visitors passed this spot. Apart from the cemetery, Granezza, in 1994, consisted of no more than a decaying mountain inn. Only the sound at lunchtimes of local farmers and their families enjoying their picnics at the gravesides punctuated the perpetual clanging of cattle bells.

Edward's grave was quickly spotted. A white oblong headstone close to the thick rubble wall bears the simple inscription, 'Captain Edward H. Brittain M.C. Notts & Derby Regiment. 15th June 1918. Aged 22'

We laid down the flowers we had brought with us, and returned to the road to catch the bus.

Chronology

1855 Thomas Brittain, Vera Brittain's great-grandfather, purchases the Ivy House Paper Mill, in Hanley, North Staffordshire, which later combines with another Staffordshire paper mill at Cheddleton, in Leek, to form the company Brittains Limited.

1864 (Thomas) Arthur Brittain, Vera's father, born.

1868 Edith Mary Bervon, Vera's mother, born.

1891 (Thomas) Arthur Brittain and Edith Bervon married.

1893 (29 December) Birth of Vera Mary Brittain at Atherstone House, Sidmouth Avenue, Newcastle-under-Lyme, North Staffordshire.

1895 (5 March) Birth of Geoffrey Robert Youngman Thurlow; (18 March) birth of Victor Richardson; (27 March) birth of Roland Aubrey Leighton; (30 November) birth of Edward Harold Brittain at 'Glen Bank', 170 Chester Road, Macclesfield, Cheshire.

1905 The Brittain family moves to Buxton, in Derbyshire.

1907 Vera is sent to St Monica's School, Kingswood, Surrey.

1908 Edward starts at Uppingham School, Rutland.

1911 (December) Vera leaves St Monica's and returns home to Buxton.

1913 (January) Vera begins attending John Marriott's University Extension Lectures at Buxton; (June) Vera meets Roland Leighton for the first time at the

Uppingham School 'Old Boys'; (September) Vera rejects a proposal of marriage from Bertram Spafford; (November) Vera starts following the controversy at Fairfield concerning the Reverend Ward.

1914 (March) Vera is awarded an exhibition in English Literature by Somerville College, Oxford; (April) Roland stays with the Brittains at Buxton; (11 July) the Uppingham School Speech Day; (4 August) the outbreak of war; (September) Roland is acting recruitment officer at Lowestoft; (October) Vera goes up to Somerville; Roland enlists as a second lieutenant in the 4th Norfolks; (November) Edward is gazetted as a second lieutenant in the 10th Sherwood Foresters, Victor in the 4th Sussex Regiment; (30–31 December) Vera meets Roland in London.

1915 (January) Geoffrey leaves University College, Oxford, after a term, to enlist as a second lieutenant in the 10th Sherwood Foresters; (March) Roland visits Vera at Buxton before leaving for the Front with the 7th Worcesters; (June) Vera takes Pass Mods before going down from Oxford in order to nurse as an auxiliary at Buxton's Devonshire Hospital; (18–27 August) Roland on leave in England; (October) Vera begins nursing as a VAD at the First London General Hospital in Camberwell; (November) Geoffrey goes to the Front with the 10th Sherwood Foresters; (22–23 December) Roland is wounded while leading an expedition to repair the barbed wire in front of trenches at Hébuterne, and dies at the Casualty Clearing Station at Louvencourt; (26 December) at the Grand Hotel in

Brighton, Vera learns of Roland's death while waiting for him to come home on leave.

1916 (February) Edward departs for the Front with the 11th Sherwood Foresters; Geoffrey suffers shell shock and a face wound during heavy bombardment at Ypres; (February–March) Vera visits Geoffrey in hospital at Fishmongers' Hall at London Bridge; (June) Edward returns to England on leave and warns of a pending great battle; (1 July) Edward is wounded on the first day of the Battle of the Somme leading the first wave of his company's attack, and is sent to Vera's hospital at Camberwell; (August) Geoffrey returns to France; Edward is awarded the Military Cross; (24 September–6 October) Vera sails to Malta to nurse at St George's Hospital; (late September) Victor transfers to the 9th King's Royal Rifles and leaves for France.

1917 (9 April) Victor is badly wounded during an attack at Arras and (19 April) arrives in England for treatment at the Second London General Hospital in Chelsea; (23 April) Geoffrey is killed in action at Monchy-le-Preux; (1 May) Vera in Malta receives two cablegrams from England, the first tells her that Victor's sight is gone, the second informs her of Geoffrey's death; (28 May) Vera arrives back in England; (9 June) Victor dies in hospital and is buried at Hove; (30 June) Edward returns to the Front; (August) Vera begins nursing at the 24 General at Etaples; (November) Edward is posted, with the 11th Sherwood Foresters, to the Italian Front in northern Italy.

1918 (January) Vera and Edward on leave together in London; (March–April) Vera nurses at Etaples during Ludendorff's great offensive; (end of April) Vera returns home to Oakwood Court to care for her parents; (15 June) Edward is killed in action during a counter-attack against the Austrian Offensive on the Asiago Plateau; (22 June) Vera and her father receive the telegram containing the news of Edward's death; (August) Vera's first book, *Verses of a V.A.D.*, is published by Erskine Macdonald; (11 November) Vera is working as a VAD in London, at Queen Alexandra's Hospital on Millbank, when the Armistice is declared.

1919 (end of April) Vera returns to Somerville College, Oxford, and changes subject to history; (October) Vera meets Winifred Holtby at a shared tutorial with the Dean of Hertford.

1921 (August–September) Vera and Winifred spend six weeks together in Italy and France after leaving Oxford, and visit Edward's grave at Granezza, and Roland's at Louvencourt; (December) Vera and Winifred move into a studio flat at 52 Doughty Street in London.

1922 Vera enters an edited version of her war diary, 'A Chronicle of Youth', in a publisher's competition for the best diary or autobiography. The diary is not chosen.

1923 Vera's first novel, *The Dark Tide*, is published in Britain by Grant Richards.

1925 (27 June) Vera marries George Catlin at St James's, Spanish Place, London.

1927 (December) John Edward Jocelyn Brittain-Catlin is born.

1929 (November) Vera begins writing *Testament of Youth*.

1930 (July) Shirley Vivian Brittain-Catlin is born.

1933 (February) Vera finishes writing *Testament of Youth*; (28 August) *Testament of Youth* is published in Britain by Gollancz; (October) the book is published by Macmillan in the United States.

1935 (August) Arthur Brittain, Vera's father, commits suicide in London by drowning; (29 September) Winifred Holtby dies in a nursing home in London from Bright's disease.

1937 (January) Vera becomes a sponsor of the pacifist organisation, the Peace Pledge Union.

1940 (January) *Testament of Friendship*, Vera's biography of Winifred Holtby, is published in Britain by Macmillan.

1944 *Seed of Chaos. What Mass Bombing Really Means*, Vera's appeal against the Allies' saturation bombing of German cities, is published in Britain by the Bombing Restriction Committee. The American edition, under the title *Massacre by Bombing*, provokes widespread attacks against Vera throughout the United States.

1957 *Testament of Experience*, Vera's autobiographical sequel to *Testament of Youth*, covering the years 1925 to 1950, is published in Britain by Gollancz.

1970 (29 March) Vera dies in a nursing home at 15 Oakwood Road, Wimbledon; (September) Vera's ashes are scattered on her brother Edward's grave at Granezza in northern Italy.

1978 (April) *Testament of Youth* is reissued by Virago Press.

1979 (7 February) Death of Sir George Catlin; (November–December) the first broadcast, on BBC Two, of Elaine

Morgan's five-part television adaptation of *Testament of Youth*, starring Cheryl Campbell as Vera Brittain (the series is repeated on BBC One the following August, and, later, on BBC Two in October 1992, as part of a 'War and Peace' season).

1980 (October) The first performance, at London's Covent Garden, of Kenneth MacMillan's ballet *Gloria*, to music by Francis Poulenc. The ballet is inspired by *Testament of Youth*, particularly the book's opening poem, 'The War Generation: Ave', written by Vera Brittain in 1932.

1981 *Chronicle of Youth*, a selection from Vera Brittain's First World War diary, edited by Alan Bishop, is published in Britain by Gollancz.

1995 *Vera Brittain: A Life*, the authorised biography by Paul Berry and Mark Bostridge, is published in Britain by Chatto & Windus.

1998 *Letters from a Lost Generation*, a selection of the First World War Letters of Vera Brittain, Roland Leighton, Edward Brittain, Victor Richardson and Geoffrey Thurlow, edited by Alan Bishop and Mark Bostridge, is published in Britain by Little, Brown to mark the 80th anniversary of the Armistice. An adaptation of the *Letters* in 15 episodes by Mark Bostridge, starring Amanda Root as Vera Brittain and Rupert Graves as Roland Leighton, is broadcast on BBC Radio Four.

2008 *Vera Brittain: A Woman in Love and War*, a BBC-TV drama-documentary, presented by Jo Brand, is broadcast on Remembrance Sunday, to mark the 90th anniversary of the end of the First World War.

2015 Release of the BBC Films/Heyday Films production of *Testament of Youth*, starring Alicia Vikander as Vera Brittain and Kit Harington as Roland Leighton.

Gazetteer of Places Associated with Vera Brittain and *Testament of Youth*

ENGLAND

NEWCASTLE-UNDER-LYME, STAFFORDSHIRE

Atherstone House, 9 Sidmouth Avenue. This semi-detached villa, with a black and white frontage, was the birthplace of Vera Brittain in December 1893 (and is commemorated by a local plaque).

MACCLESFIELD, CHESHIRE

'Glen Bank', 170 Chester Road. The Brittain family moved from Newcastle-under-Lyme to this large, semi-detached house in the summer of 1895, and remained here for ten years. Edward Brittain was born at 'Glen Bank' in November 1895.

BUXTON, DERBYSHIRE

'Melrose', 151 The Park. The second Buxton home occupied by the Brittain family following their move to the town in 1905 (the first, High Leigh, was in Manchester Road). They took a lease on this 'tall, grey, stone house' in 1907 and stayed there until late 1915, when Mr Brittain retired early from the paper mill. Vera Brittain lived at 'Melrose' until October 1915, when she moved to London to begin nursing as a VAD nurse at the First London General Hospital in Camberwell. A blue plaque on the house, now divided into three flats, commemorates her time at 'Melrose' (though the plaque gives the wrong year – 1914 – for her departure).

The Town Hall. In January 1913, Vera Brittain began attending a course of University Extension Lectures given by John Marriott at the Town Hall. This led to her decision to try for Oxford University later that year.

St Peter's Church, Fairfield. In 1913–14, Vera Brittain paid regular visits to this church at Fairfield, a small village to the east of Buxton, to listen to the sermons of the young Anglican curate, Joseph Harry Ward. On various occasions she was accompanied by her mother, Edward Brittain and Roland Leighton.

Devonshire Hospital. Converted in 1859 into a convalescent hospital from the Duke of Devonshire's riding school and stables, the Devonshire possesses a circular area of half-an-acre covered by the world's largest unsupported dome. Vera Brittain worked here as a nursing assistant from the end of June to the last week of September 1915.

Today the former hospital forms part of the University of Derby and of Buxton College.

Devonshire Hospital

Buxton War Memorial. Commemorating residents of the town who died in both World Wars, the memorial is to be found on The Slopes, a steep landscaped hill in the centre of Buxton, situated opposite the eighteenth-century Crescent. Edward Brittain's is one of 314 names from the First World War.

RUTLAND

Uppingham School, Uppingham. The public school, founded in the sixteenth century, attended by Edward Brittain, Roland Leighton and Victor Richardson. Their names, together with those of 474 other Uppinghamians killed in the war, are listed on the walls of the school's memorial chapel.

OXFORD

Somerville College, Woodstock Road. Founded in 1879, Somerville was one of the four women's colleges of Oxford University in 1914. Vera Brittain went up to Somerville in October that year, occupying a room in the Maitland Building. At the beginning of Trinity (summer) Term 1915, she moved to a room at Micklem Hall, off St Aldate's (now demolished and the site of the present day Campion Hall), following the War Office's requisition of Somerville's buildings as a military hospital. Half of Somerville was accommodated in the St Mary Hall Quadrangle at Oriel College, the rest in various 'outhouses'.

A Brittain-Williams room, commemorating Vera Brittain, and associating her name with that of her daughter, the politician Shirley Williams, up at Somerville from 1948 to 1951, was opened at the college in November 2013.

Merton College, Merton Street. Although his enlistment in 1914 meant that Roland Leighton never studied at Merton, where he had been awarded a Senior Open Classical Postmastership, his name is one of those on the College's War Memorial.

University College, High Street. Geoffrey Thurlow was an undergraduate at University College for a single term only, from October to December 1914, before he left Oxford to enlist. His name is on the War Memorial in the College Chapel.

CAMBRIDGE

Emmanuel College, St Andrew's Street. But for the war, Victor Richardson would have studied medicine at Emmanuel College. His name is included on the College War Memorial.

LOWESTOFT

'Heather Cliff', Gunton Cliff, Lowestoft. The Leighton family home, to the north of the town, high up overlooking the North Sea, which Vera Brittain visited with Roland Leighton while he was on leave in August 1915. Originally the family's summer home, it became their permanent base in 1913 after they gave up their London house at 40 Abbey Road, St John's Wood. However, the Leightons did not remain at Lowestoft for much longer. In late 1915 they rented a cottage at **2 The Crescent, Keymer, Hassocks, West Sussex**. It was at Keymer, in December 1915, that they received the news of Roland's death, and where, in January 1916, they buried his uniform in the back garden.

A plaque on the east side of 'Heather Cliff' commemorates its association with *Testament of Youth*.

LONDON

St Pancras Station, Euston Road. Designed by George Gilbert Scott, and built in 1866–77 by the Midland Railway Company as its London terminus, this Gothic revival masterpiece was the place of reunion for Vera Brittain and Roland Leighton on his leave in August 1915. It also provided the setting, on 23 August, for their final farewell, as Roland saw Vera off on her train back to Buxton to resume her work at the Devonshire Hospital.

First London General Hospital, Cormont Road, Camberwell, SE5. The first military hospital at which Vera Brittain nursed, from October 1915 to August 1916. Among her patients was Edward Brittain, who arrived as a patient at Camberwell in July 1916 during the aftermath of the first day of the Battle of the Somme.

The hospital was converted from a teachers' training college called St Gabriel's College for Ladies, while the

First London General Hospital, Camberwell

neighbouring Cormont Secondary School served as a hospital for convalescent cases (the two buildings were connected by a long covered passage).

In December 1915, huts to accommodate a further 520 patients were erected in the park opposite, known as **Myatt's Fields Park**. By 1917, the hospital contained 231 beds for officers and 1,038 for other ranks.

Today the main hospital building is St Gabriel's Manor, an apartment block within a gated development.

Second London General Hospital, 552 King's Road, Chelsea, SW10. This hospital, where Victor Richardson was cared for in the optical ward, and where he died in June 1917, was also originally a teachers' training college, called St Mark's College (an adjoining LCC secondary school formed the surgical section). A wall at the west side of the grounds was partially demolished to allow access to platforms at nearby Chelsea station, so that patients could be transferred from the ambulance trains directly to the hospital by the shortest and most private route.

From 1915, all patients with badly damaged eyes were sent to the Second London General (or, if it was full, to the Third London General, in Wandsworth). Staff from St Dunstan's Hostel for Blinded Soldiers and Sailors visited blinded servicemen to help the newly-blind cope with the depression that generally followed the loss of sight.

Fishmongers' Hall, London Bridge, EC4. Owned by one of the 12 ancient Great Livery Companies of the

City of London, Fishmongers' Hall was opened as a hospital for officers in October 1914. The Great Hall, with its gilded walls and ceiling, and the other apartments on the first floor of the building, were subdivided by wooden partitions to form cubicles. Each cubicle had a home-like atmosphere, with two armchairs, a reading table and an electric light. Patients were permitted to entertain two guests for afternoon tea. The hospital never had more than thirty beds.

Vera Brittain visited Geoffrey Thurlow here on three occasions in February and March 1916 while he was recovering from shell-shock and a slight face wound.

10 Oakwood Court, Kensington, W14. The flat, close to Kensington High Street, to which the Brittains moved in 1916 (after first settling in number 8, a larger one in the same block). It was here, on 22 June 1918, that Vera Brittain and her father received the telegram notifying them of Edward Brittain's death in action on the Asiago Plateau on 15 June.

52 Doughty Street, Bloomsbury, WC1. Vera Brittain and Winifred Holtby occupied a studio flat here, their first home together, from December 1921 to September 1922, at which point they moved to a more spacious top-floor flat at **58 Doughty Street**, where a blue plaque commemorates their time at the address. In November 1923, they moved again to a large, unfurnished flat at **117 Wymering Mansions, Wymering Road, Maida Vale, W9** (a green Westminster City Council plaque marks

Vera Brittain's residence here). They continued to rent the flat until September 1927.

19 Glebe Place, Chelsea, SW3. Vera Brittain's home from April 1930 to May 1937, where she lived with her husband George Catlin, their children John and Shirley, and Winifred Holtby. Most of *Testament of Youth* was written here, as were parts of Winifred Holtby's final, posthumously published, novel, *South Riding*.

BRIGHTON AND HOVE, EAST SUSSEX

The Grand Hotel, Brighton. This opulent Victorian hotel, situated on Brighton's seafront, was where Vera Brittain learned of Roland Leighton's death, on 26 December 1915. He had died on 23 December after receiving gunshot wounds to his stomach during a night time inspection of the barbed wire in front of a trench a day earlier.

Hove (Old) Cemetery, Old Shoreham Road, Hove. Burial place of Victor Richardson (grave reference H.A. 56). Victor Richardson died on 9 June 1917 at the Second London General Hospital in Chelsea, from wounds sustained during the Battle of Arras on 9 April.

Victor Richardson's name is on the **Hove War Memorial** in the entrance to the **Public Library, 182–186 Church Street, Hove**. His name is also commemorated on a plaque at the Richardson family's parish church, **St Barnabas, Sackville Road, Hove**, alongside the names of the two other Uppingham musketeers, Roland Leighton and Edward Brittain.

ESSEX

Chigwell School, High Road, Chigwell. Geoffrey Thurlow is one of 79 former pupils of the school commemorated on its War Memorial (his older brother, John, killed on 24 April 1918 – almost a year to the day of Geoffrey's death – is also commemorated here). The names of both brothers are inscribed on the lych gate War Memorial of their parish church, **St John's, Buckhurst Hill**, and on their parents' grave in the churchyard.

BELGIUM

Ploegsteert Wood. Known colloquially among British troops as 'Plug Street Wood'. The small village of Ploegsteert, and its nearby wood, are two miles south of Armentières, eight miles south of Ypres, and close to the French border. On 17 April 1915, Roland Leighton's battalion took over a stretch of trenches in Ploegsteert Wood, and remained there for almost three months, with periods out of the line. The British had wrested the area from German control in November 1914, though it was still subject to regular shell and rifle fire from the German lines, 70 to 180 yards away. It was here, on 25 April, that Roland completed his Villanelle, 'Violets', which he showed to Vera Brittain later that summer.

By the roadside today, adjacent to the wood, is an information panel giving the names of well-known people who served in this area. Roland Leighton is among them.

Ploegsteert Wood and Ploegsteert village

FRANCE

Louvencourt. A village 13 kilometres to the south-east of Doullens, on the road to Albert, on the Somme. The **military cemetery**, one of the first of three Commonwealth Graves Commission cemeteries to be built after the First World War, from a design by Sir

Reginald Blomfield, is on the south-eastern side of the village. There are 151 Commonwealth burials of the First World War at Louvencourt, and 76 French war graves, dating from 1915 (the cemetery also contains three graves from the Second World War).

Roland Leighton's grave is at Plot 1, Row B, Grave 20. His headstone, with its quotation from 'Echoes XLII', a short poem by W. E. Henley, gives Roland's age as 19, although he was in fact 20.

Vera Brittain made two visits to Roland's grave, on both occasions accompanied by Winifred Holtby, the first in October 1921, the second in the summer of 1933, shortly before the publication of *Testament of Youth*. Edward Brittain had visited the grave in April 1916, before the construction of the cemetery.

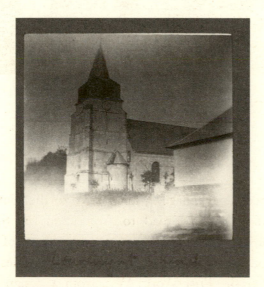

Louvencourt Church

The church, where Roland's military funeral was held on 26 December 1915, is nearby. The eighteenth-century **Château de Louvencourt**, a casualty clearing station in 1915, where Roland was operated on and died, is just to the north of the church.

Faubourg d'Amiens Cemetery, Boulevard de General de Gaulle, in the western part of the town of Arras, has a **Memorial to the Missing**. This includes Geoffrey Thurlow's name (on Bay 7) as one of almost 35,000 servicemen from Great Britain, South Africa and New Zealand, who died in the Arras sector between the spring of 1916 and 7 August 1918, and have no known grave.

24 General Hospital, Etaples. Today, the vast Commonwealth military cemetery, to the north of the town, designed by Lutyens, and containing 10,771 burials from the First World War, covers part of the site of the British wartime hospital and reinforcement camp. The site of the 24 General, where Vera Brittain nursed from 1917–18, is to be found among a small group of modern houses in the Avenue du Blanc Pavé.

Etaples Hospitals, before bombardment May 1918

7. - ETAPLES-sur-MER (P.-de C.). - Chantiers de Constructions

Etaples

MALTA

St George's Hospital, St George's Bay. The hospital where Vera Brittain nursed in 1916–17 was a converted British Army barracks (it reverted to its original purpose after the war). This was demolished some time after the Second World War. Today the bay is dominated by a modern hotel, but it is still possible to see remains of some of the barrack buildings and outhouses, which are currently in use as flats. The rocks on the seafront where Vera Brittain sat in April 1917, and decided to go home to marry Victor Richardson, are also clearly identifiable.

St George's Hospital

ITALY

Granezza, a village 9 kilometres south of the town of Asiago in the commune of Lusiana, in the Veneto region of northern Italy. The **British military cemetery** is one of five cemeteries situated on the Asiago Plateau. It contains 142 First World War burials, including those of three unknown British soldiers.

Edward Brittain's grave is at Plot 1, Row B, Grave 1.

Vera Brittain visited Edward's grave, accompanied by Winifred Holtby, in September 1921, and again, in the summer of 1925, with George Catlin. In September 1970, five months after her death, Vera Brittain's ashes were scattered on her brother's grave.

Granezza Cenotaph

Further Reading

Vera Brittain's *Testament of Youth. An Autobiographical Study of the Years 1900-1925*, first published in 1933, is available in a modern critical edition, with a preface by Shirley Williams and an introduction by Mark Bostridge, published in paperback by Virago, and in hardback by Weidenfeld and Nicolson.

The published selections from Vera Brittain's diaries and letters used throughout this book are:

Chronicle of Youth. War Diary 1913-1917, edited by Alan Bishop with Terry Smart (1981).
Letters from a Lost Generation. First World War Letters of Vera Brittain and Four Friends, edited by Alan Bishop and Mark Bostridge (1998).

The modern critical edition of Vera Brittain's war poetry is:

Because You Died. Poetry and Prose of the First World War and After, edited and introduced by Mark Bostridge (2008).

Quotations from unpublished sections of the complete diary have been taken from the typed transcript of the diary in the Vera Brittain Collection at Somerville College, Oxford.

Unpublished letters and other manuscripts form part of the Vera Brittain Archive in the William Ready Division of Archives and Research Collections at McMaster University, Hamilton, Ontario.

The standard biography of Vera Brittain is *Vera Brittain: A Life* by Paul Berry and Mark Bostridge (1995), which includes a detailed bibliography. This may be usefully supplemented by *Vera Brittain. A Feminist Life* by Deborah Gorham (1996) which traces the development of Vera Brittain's feminist beliefs, and has a number of interesting points to make about the ways in which the autobiographical account in *Testament of Youth* distorts Vera Brittain's experience of the First World War.

Roland Leighton

Clare Leighton's *Tempestuous Petticoat. The Story of an Invincible Edwardian* (1947) is a vivid portrait of her mother Marie Leighton and of the Leighton family. Marie Leighton's *Boy of My Heart*, her posthumous memoir of Roland, published anonymously in 1916, can now be read online at https://archive.org/stream/boyofmyheartoonewyrich/ (accessed 21 August 2014).

Harry Ricketts's *Strange Meetings. The Poets of the Great War* (2010) has a useful chapter on the relationship between Vera Brittain and Roland Leighton viewed mainly from the perspective of their poetry.

None That Go Return. Leighton, Brittain and Friends and the Lost Generation 1914-18 by Don Farr (2010) contains biographical minutiae relating to Roland, Edward, Victor and Geoffrey.

The Old Lie. The Great War and the Public School Ethos by Peter Parker (1987) is a good starting point for consideration of public school militarism in 1914. C. R. W. Nevinson, *Paint and Prejudice* (1937), gives a jaundiced view of Uppingham School, where Nevinson was a pupil from 1904 to 1907 (he left early because of bullying).

Oxford

Somerville for Women. An Oxford College 1879-1993 by Pauline Adams (1996) provides historical background for Vera Brittain's time at Somerville.

Vera Brittain's *The Dark Tide* (1923, reprinted 1999) is a *roman à clef*, which offers a thinly disguised account of Vera Brittain's return to Somerville after the war.

VADs, First World War nurses and hospitals

Lyn Macdonald's *The Roses of No Man's Land* (1980) is a pioneering study, using first-hand testimony, of the British volunteer nurses of the First World War.

The relevant chapter in Sharon Ouditt, *Fighting Forces, Writing Women. Identity and Ideology in the First World War* (1994), looks at the experiences of Voluntary

Aid Detachment nurses and the ways in which they were portrayed in writing.

Janet S. K. Watson, *Fighting Different Wars. Experience, Memory, and the First World War in Britain* (2004) considers the relations between trained and amateur nurses during the war.

The website 'Lost Hospitals of London' (http://ezitis.myzen.co.uk/index.html, accessed 21 August 2014) contains many interesting details about London hospitals, including the First London General, Camberwell, during the First World War.

Douglas Gill, in his article 'No Compromise with Truth. Vera Brittain 1917', *Krug Und Literatur*, V, 1999, 67–95, first identified the discrepancies in Vera Brittain's account of her nursing at Etaples. The official records of the 24 General at Etaples, covering Vera Brittain's time there, are in the National Archives, WO 95/4085.

War books and the writing of *Testament of Youth*

All the manuscripts of the early versions of *Testament of Youth* are preserved in the Vera Brittain Archive at McMaster University.

There are interesting discussions of War books, and the controversies they inspired, which I have drawn on here, in: Gary Sheffield, *Forgotten Victory. The First World War: Myths and Realities* (2001); Hugh Cecil, *The Flower of Battle. British Fiction Writers of the First World War* (1995), which includes a chapter on R. H. Mottram, and the *Spanish Farm Trilogy*; Samuel Hynes, *A War Imagined*.

The First World War and English Culture (1990); and Janet S. K. Watson, *Fighting Different Wars. Experience, Memory, and the First World War in Britain* (2004).

Women's Writing on the First World War, edited by Agnes Cardinal, Dorothy Goldman and Judith Hattaway (1999) contains interesting extracts from a large number of female writers, including Mary Borden. Claire M. Tylee, *The Great War and Women's Consciousness. Images of Militarism and Womanhood in Women's Writings, 1914-64* (1990), includes an extensive bibliography of women's writings about the war.

Biographical material about the writing of *Testament of Youth* can be found in *Selected Letters of Winifred Holtby and Vera Brittain*, edited by Vera Brittain and Geoffrey Handley-Taylor (1960); and in *Chronicle of Friendship. Vera Brittain's Diary of the Thirties 1932-1939*, edited by Alan Bishop (1986).

Phyllis Bentley's unpublished diary is housed in the Calderdale section of West Yorkshire Archives Department, Calderdale Central Library, Halifax (PB/C/14/1). For a description of the parts of it relating to Vera Brittain, see Dave Russell, 'Province, Metropolis, and the Literary Career of Phyllis Bentley in the 1930s', *The Historical Journal*, 51, 3, 2008, 719–40.

Some of the best literary critical analysis of *Testament of Youth*, which I have drawn on, is by Jean E. Kennard in *Vera Brittain and Winifred Holtby. A Working Partnership* (1989).

The myth of the lost generation is analysed in demographic terms by J. M. Winter in *The Great War and the British People* (1985).

Dramatisations

BBC Television's five-part adaptation of *Testament of Youth* (1979) is available on DVD from Acorn Media (2010).

For background to the 1979 television series, see the article by Philippa Toomey, 'Vera Brittain and the Testament that came late to life', *The Times*, 9 August 1980.

BBC Radio Four's 15-part adaptation of *Letters from a Lost Generation* is available on CD from BBC Audio (2014).

Rachel Beaumont's article (2014) on 'The Personal Inspiration behind Kenneth MacMillan's *Gloria*' can be found online at http://www.roh.org.uk/news/the-personal-tragedy-that-inspired-kenneth-macmillans-gloria (accessed 21 August 2014).

Index